KILLER TRIGGERS

ALSO BY JOE KENDA

I WILL FIND YOU:
Solving Killer Cases from My Life Fighting Crime

JOE KENDA

KILLER TRIGGERS

BLACK STONE
PUBLISHING

Please note that the names of certain individuals in
this book have been changed to protect their identities.
Most of them were innocents whose lives were caught
up in horrendous crimes through no fault of their own.
Others were given pseudonyms because they never
were convicted of a crime even if they weren't
exactly babes in the woods.

Printed in the United States of America

First edition: 2021
ISBN 978-1-982678-35-7
True Crime / Murder / General

1 3 5 7 9 10 8 6 4 2

CIP data for this book is available
from the Library of Congress

Blackstone Publishing
31 Mistletoe Rd.
Ashland, OR 97520

www.BlackstonePublishing.com

I dedicate this book to my wife, Kathy;
our son, Dan; and our daughter, Kris,
because they were kind enough to stand by me over the years
despite the toll taken by my career in pursuit of killers. I'm doing my best
to make it up to them by sharing in the rewards of my more recent—unlikely
and totally unexpected—second career as a true-crime
television show host and author.

CONTENTS

CHAPTER ONE:
A RUNNER'S FATAL WALK

THE TRIGGER: MONEY

Once I became the lieutenant in charge of the homicide division, my role was like that of a symphony conductor. I'd walk into the scene of a murder and try to pick up on the melody so that I could orchestrate the investigation.

My team of detectives were like symphony musicians. They each had distinct talents and levels of experience. My job was to get them to work in harmony. Sometimes, things went smoothly. Other times, we'd have to stop and start over, maybe even more than once.

As the conductor, I had to monitor our progress and make sure we were all in tune and in sync while moving toward a resolution. Murder investigations rarely compare to beautiful music. They are more like a cacophony of clashing notes, but it is in the clashing that crimes are solved—clashing alibis, clashing eyewitness reports, and clashing interrogations.

We didn't like complications, but we were very good at sorting things out. This case from 1993 had many complications. It began when our 911 operators received a call from an east-side laundromat operator who reported that a customer had found a man shot in a nearby shopping center parking lot.

"A lady came in and told us we should come outside, and we saw a woman bent over an older man giving him CPR and screaming, 'Breathe, motherfucker! Breathe!'" the caller said.

Our officers rushed to the scene and found an older man dressed in pink running shorts, a red T-shirt, and fancy running shoes. He had been shot once. The small-caliber bullet passed through his left arm and into his chest. Although he had been breathing when the woman found him, he died shortly after our EMTs took him to the hospital.

His wallet and its contents were intact, and his driver's license identified him as Robert Elshire, seventy-one, of Heber Springs, Arkansas. My guys also found a card from a local executive-suites hotel, room 2G, which was within walking distance of the crime scene.

I sent a couple of detectives over to check it out.

As these initial reports came in, I tapped my baton and asked my team of detectives to answer the first flurry of questions that came to mind:

Who killed Robert Elshire, and why?

What was this midwestern guy even doing in my town?

And what the hell was the deal with the dozens of neon-colored packets of condoms scattered all around the crime scene and along the killer's apparent flight path?

We've found a lot of crazy stuff at crime scenes, but the six-months' supply of condoms was a strange twist. At that point, we had no idea whether they were connected to the murder.

We rounded up several witnesses who had seen two young males, one Black and one Black or Hispanic, running from the parking lot after the shooting. One woman was driving by when the two suspects ran from the scene. She had to hit the brakes to avoid hitting one of them. She got a good look at him, saying he'd worn a bandanna over his face and gray pants.

Several others in the area heard Mr. Elshire yelling before a shot was fired. Then they heard a younger man scream out before running away and joining another across the street.

Early indications were that Mr. Elshire might have resisted during an attempted robbery. We would soon learn that this World War II veteran, union electrician, and fitness enthusiast wasn't easily intimidated. He was a strong, tough guy, but he'd taken a bullet directly to his heart. It had passed through his left arm and into his chest, where it punctured his lung, passed through his heart, and lodged in his spine.

BREAKING BAD NEWS

There is no easy way to break the news to the family of a murder victim. We receive no training for it, but we take it upon ourselves to do it as gently as possible. Otherwise, the coroner would do it, and that was the worst possibility. They'd just call family members and say, "Your son is dead." It was that cold.

I always tried to soften the blow somehow, which was futile most of the time. The heart never heals from this sort of tragedy.

As a homicide detective, all too often you find yourself standing on the front porch, in a cheap suit and holding a badge, and then the door opens and you can see it on their faces. Someone is not home who should be home. They haven't heard from a family member who usually calls. They know it's coming, and you have to be the bearer of the worst news they'll ever hear.

I'm very sorry to inform you that your (fill in the blank) is no longer alive.

I never said "killed" or "murdered," because those words are like bullets. I'd just say they were no longer alive, and wait for the reaction. I've seen all types. Some people just stare at you. Some laugh nervously. Some scream, or collapse, or punch the messenger.

I always told my guys just to do it quickly, gently, and as simply as possible, and then be prepared for anything and everything in response. You just never know whether the loved ones will collapse on you, turn on you, or throw you out the door. In another murder investigation, when we told a woman her husband had been killed, she grabbed a rookie detective's tie and went down, yanking him to the ground and nearly strangling the poor guy.

In this case, our detectives pulled into the hotel parking lot and saw a woman on the balcony outside room 2G. She looked distraught, especially after she spotted their car.

"That must be his wife, looking for him," one of our detectives told the other.

Helen Elshire opened the apartment door with her hand in front of her mouth.

"Oh, God, what has happened to my husband!"

One detective embraced her immediately because he was afraid she might collapse in grief.

"Your husband was shot in an apparent robbery attempt," he told her.

She slumped against the hallway wall. Her knees buckled, so our detective held her tighter. She convulsed with sobs and moans.

"How bad is he hurt?" she asked.

"I'm afraid he did not survive the gunshot wound to his chest," the detective said.

You won't often see a television or movie detective serving as a compassionate grief counselor, but that is part of the job, too. Some are better at it than others, of course, and this detective was a very empathetic guy.

He waited patiently for Mrs. Elshire to gather herself, at least momentarily, and then he offered to help her reach out to other members of the immediate family. He knew that the poor woman needed to do it before he could question her.

In this case, our guy went above and beyond. He even helped Mrs. Elshire find her family phone book and stood by while she called several relatives. He later arranged for a police chaplain and members of the Senior Victim Assistance Team to talk with them and to stay with Mrs. Elshire that night since she had no family members in town.

Spouses and other family members have been known to die of grief upon losing a loved one. We did not want that to happen.

Mrs. Elshire's mourning was all the deeper because, as she told us that night, her husband had left the safety of their hotel room to go to the Walgreens to get her some antacid pills for her upset stomach.

We had found them and a local newspaper in a paper bag alongside his body.

Mrs. Elshire also told us that she and her husband had come to town just a couple of days earlier.

"He wanted to run in the Pikes Peak Marathon one more time," said his wife of forty-eight years. "He'd run it four times in the past, sat out a couple years, and planned on making this his last trip up the mountain."

THE TRIGGER

Robert Elshire was a very fit man for his age, but the single gunshot had done extensive damage once it entered his chest. Smaller-caliber bullets tend to ricochet around inside the body, while more powerful rounds will go straight through. If the larger-caliber bullet doesn't hit any vital organs, chances of survival are pretty good. That's not the case with the less powerful ammunition commonly carried by young street criminals.

They are more concerned about protecting themselves than hurting anyone else. They get these Saturday night specials on the cheap. Most are traded, stolen, and passed around constantly. We always figured if a gun was stolen in a burglary, it would change hands at least ten times in the first two days. Trying to control their movement is a fantasy. There are too many of them out there already, and they aren't owned by law-abiding citizens.

Armed robbers wave a gun in the face of their targets to scare them into complying. They don't usually intend to shoot them, but if the victim fails to comply, resists, or somehow "disrespects" them, they may fire out of fear.

Yeah, it's crazy, but that's the way these idiots think. And they've got the gun, so it's their way or else. If you don't make a move that scares them—or insult their sensitive souls—and just hand over your wallet and watch or whatever, you have a decent chance of avoiding injury or death.

Maybe. Don't hold me to that.

The other danger is that the trigger pulls on those cheap guns are very light. Many automatically cock when a bullet is in the chamber, and you can't tell whether it's cocked by looking at it. Not that many of these brainless street bandits ever had any gun training, which makes them all the more dangerous with these cheap weapons.

They don't train, and they don't plan. They just grab a gun, walk up to a stranger, and demand cash. These robbers did not plot this out over several weeks or days—or even hours. They couldn't plan a party of one.

That's the sad part of this. The Elshire family lost their patriarch, by all accounts a good man, because a couple of dopes needed rent money, booze money, or drug money.

DUMB AND DUMBER GET AXED

Now, you may think me cruel and disparaging to label our two suspects "dopes," but within just a few hours after killing a beloved husband, father, and upstanding person, they proved themselves to be dopes of the first order. If they had simply holed up somewhere or found a way to get the hell out of town, we might never have nabbed them.

Instead, the bozos returned to the scene of their crime, which usually happens only on television shows like *CSI Dubuque*. Okay, it does happen from time to time, which is why we always keep an eye on any crowd gathered around a crime scene.

We do the same at funerals and burials. If we have reason to believe the killer might show up, we'll have a guy tucked away in a van or behind a tree, taking videos and photos. Sometimes, perps feel remorse and have this strange need to apologize or at least show they're sorry. Not every killer is cold-blooded. Some are capable of remorse.

Others may just want to see the person they killed put into the ground. More twisted killers may want to see the family and friends grieving. This is particularly true in arson cases. Arsonists are known to enjoy watching the suffering and horror they created.

We do surveillance and, afterward, go over the video and the photos, trying to identify everyone there. On occasion, we will identify a suspect at a funeral or graveside service. But that happens mostly on television.

And yet, three and a half hours into our investigation of this murder, while searching the area near the parking lot, one of our sharp-eyed K-9 patrol beasts spotted two teens on the run.

Earlier, the dog and its handler, Officer Matthews, had found more of the mystery condom packets scattered near a fence by a condominium complex. He figured they may have jumped the fence or ditched the gun nearby, so he returned to search more thoroughly.

The four-legged partner of this K-9 team was a black German shepherd named Ax—a beautiful beast who was very good at his job. He was an aggressive alpha dog and didn't take shit from anyone, human or otherwise. Most other dogs wouldn't go anywhere near him, and even Officer Matthews was a little scared of Ax.

And yet, for some reason, Ax loved me.

I found that very endearing. He really was a very smart animal. If I even just whispered his name, Ax would come running, wagging his tail.

He never wagged his tail at anyone else.

"How do you do that?" his handler would say.

"I believe we are kindred souls," I'd reply.

Officer Matthews did not disagree with that.

Ax must have felt the same way, because he was very protective of me. For example, when I took my friend Kenny on a crime scene visit one time, Ax was either jealous or sensed that Kenny was in real estate. He growled at him several times.

"What the hell kind of animal is that?" Kenny asked.

Ax had that effect on people, which was a good thing.

The giant black beast glared at Kenny as if to say, "Who the fuck are you?"

Kenny nearly shit himself.

"Just don't make any sudden moves, especially in my direction," I whispered to him. "Ax is my wingman, and he's vicious."

The entire time we were at the crime scene, Ax kept checking out Kenny, glaring at him with a look that said, "I don't know you, so watch your ass, because I sure am."

I'm a big fan of police dogs. They perform a great service, and I have no doubt that they've saved many lives. I especially loved Ax. Some said we had the same personality. I actually tried to adopt Ax when they retired him, but his hips had given out and his big heart had weakened. They had to put him down. It was very sad because that dog was a real hero.

In the Elshire case, when Officer Matthews put Ax on the trail of our suspects that night, the shepherd suddenly stopped and gave a bark alert. His handler followed the dog's line of sight and saw two young males who matched our suspects' description.

Yes, Dopey and Dopey-er had returned to the scene of their crime. It wasn't out of guilt or any desire to turn themselves in. They were just looking for the three guns they had ditched, because the gangbanger they borrowed them from wanted them back.

Apparently, they were more afraid of pissing off that guy than getting caught and sent to prison. Stupid criminals often made my job easier— just not often enough.

The two sprinted in opposite directions, but Officer Matthews cornered one of them and threatened to unleash Ax. That was all it took. Even a really stupid kid can figure out that surrendering is better than being ripped to shreds by a massive German shepherd.

Our guys swarmed the neighborhood, and the second kid quickly gave himself up, too. We cuffed them and took them in for separate interrogations.

Then the real fun began.

LIE DETECTION

One of the suspects was Allan Lucero, age seventeen. The other turned out to be Darnell E. Dimond, though he gave a fake name at first. This was not a big surprise. Young assholes on the street follow the standard juvenile-dirtbag code: "Never tell an adult the truth."

Kids begin lying to their parents shortly after they learn to speak. I've suspected that they plan their lies while still in the womb.

"No, I didn't eat that cookie. Doggie did!"

If the parents let it go, thinking it's cute or not important, the kid thinks, *I lied and it worked!*

That sort of parenting breeds the kids like those who shot Robert Elshire. That shouldn't shock you, but the parents of juveniles always seem stunned when we arrest their darlings and say, "Your child is a criminal."

The parents look at us like, "How can that be?"

Well, it is the result of parenting without penalties. If your child lies and no punishment is rendered, the lies will continue, and they will grow as the child grows. The only way to really get to a child is through fear. They must fear the consequences of bad behavior. Many people don't believe in corporal punishment, and that's fine, but your kids must at least fear your disapproval and disappointment, if nothing else.

Most of the successful people I know were spanked as kids, but they claim the thing they feared most was disappointing the parents who cared so deeply for them. Criminals rarely spring from that sort of parenting.

The people we arrest, juveniles included, likely come from broken or otherwise messed-up families, and they are practiced liars. The kids will lie out of instinct and out of self-preservation—even out of habit.

Darnell Dimond lied reflexively when Ax and his handler chased him down. They took him to a nearby police substation, where a lab tech performed a gunshot residue test on him. The kid gave the lab tech his real name at that point, forgetting his earlier lie.

We talked to him three times between 1:25 a.m. and 4:30 a.m., usually for a half hour or less. During the second meeting, Dimond asked to speak to his father. Our detective asked him his age again. He said he was eighteen, and as an adult, he didn't have the right to call in family members, and we didn't want them around that early in our interrogations into a murder case.

When we talked to him the third time, he again asked to call his father. We refused again because he still maintained that he was eighteen years old. He also told one of our guys that he had two kids.

After that third interview, we formally arrested him and told Dimond we were taking him to our adult detention facility. At that point, he claimed he was only seventeen years old. We figured he was lying again because he didn't want to go to big-boy jail, but we ran his name through the computer database, and lo and behold, we found his correct date of birth. Dimond really was two months away from his eighteenth birthday—still a juvenile in the eyes of the law.

We learned this only after the little shit had lied to us at least five times, saying he was already eighteen. Based on the crime, the law still allowed us to charge him as an adult. We locked him up for felony murder, attempted aggravated robbery, and conspiracy to commit aggravated robbery.

DUMB COP, NICE COP, SNEAKY COP

To get to the truth and file formal charges, we had to wade through a huge pile of lies spewed by both Dimond and Lucero. They danced around the truth for several hours. We interviewed them separately, of course. That's the good thing about having two suspects: you can play them and their lies against each other. I've never seen it fail with two young guys who have heard all the stories about what happens inside prison walls, where older, stronger, more powerful inmates turn them into prey.

When you interview two suspects separately, there's a lot of back-and-forth and coming and going—all part of a proven strategy. If you aren't getting anywhere with one suspect, you leave the room for a while, then come back and say, "Your friend is telling a different story, and we find it very interesting."

You then leave for a while, letting the guy stew over it. Then you play them against each other.

"Well, your friend says *you* did it, and he told us some things that checked out. So what do you say about *that!*"

I don't play tennis, handball, or racquetball. *This* was my favorite sport. And I was very good at the game, as were the detectives on my team. If you played it right, you won, and bad people were locked up or sent to an early grave.

The one thing you don't want to do during an interrogation is piss off a suspect. This makes them more likely to either clam up or lawyer up, and neither of those options furthers your investigation. Early in my career, I tended to get frustrated and blow up at them. I learned not to do that. I am trainable—just ask my wife.

After learning my lesson (probably more times than necessary), I set a new goal. I became Mr. Helpful. I became the cop who brought them a bottle of water or a cup of coffee. I played the fumbling Detective Colombo card, too. I dropped papers on the floor and forgot things, to convince them that they were much smarter than this dolt with a badge. So you could say I was an actor even before they gave me a television show.

I played a very convincing moron. Criminals are not often clever, but they are cunning. If they think you're an idiot, they'll think they can play you, and you play along while setting the trap.

Rumor has it that I've been heard to say things like: "I don't even understand why you're here. What did they arrest you for?" "I don't get it, so would you explain it to me?" "Oh, first I have to advise you of your rights, is that okay? It's just a formality."

You want the suspect to think you're just curious and trying to figure out why you are both in this awful room. Most people want to be understood, and they often will incriminate themselves while trying to explain why the person they killed deserved it, asked for it, or just mistakenly walked into a knife seventeen times.

I also used diversion to keep them off guard. Instead of asking, "Why the hell did you shoot your grandfather in the head?" I would say, "Do you have any pets? I'm a dog man myself."

Diversion questions serve a couple of purposes. They throw off a suspect who is primed to play defense or not talk to you at all. *He wants to talk about pets. I guess I can do that. Nothing against the law about owning pets, right?*

Those off-the-wall questions also take their minds off the fact that they have been arrested and taken to a police station or jail and they are now facing a potentially life-changing event. I want them to forget all that. I talk to them like the guy sitting next to them in a bar, like some curious half-drunk guy who wishes them no harm and might give them a ride home.

Another technique is to get them to repeat their stories over and over. "I forgot what you told me last time. Can you run through that again?" I do remember, of course—every single word, even if I don't write it down. I'm looking for the first lie. *Tell me a lie, because if you do, I'll know I'm talking to the right guy.*

Innocent people don't lie. And once a lie is on the table, you beat them over the head with it. "Two hours ago, you said you went somewhere else. Were you lying then? Or are you lying now?"

Once they lied to me, I could go from their best bar buddy to their worst nightmare in a split second. *This is tag, and you are it, you piece of shit!*

FLIPPING FRIENDS

Having two young suspects to work with is easier in many ways because you separate them and play them against each other. Along the way, you carefully push the buttons, leading them to think that their buddy in the other room is ratting them out. You unleash all their fears and paranoia while avoiding specifics and offering vague but ominous innuendo about the flow of information coming from the other guy.

Sometimes, I cranked up the pressure by offering colorful stories about the wonders of prison life. The swell sleeping accommodations. Bunk mates! The daily cuisine. The close camaraderie with fellow criminals. And, of course, the presence of sexual predators who are happy to make up for the lack of female companionship in their own creative ways.

Fear is in the mind, and in suspects whose partner in crime is also in custody. Their minds race with the worst possibilities. As law enforcement officers, a.k.a. the good guys, we are allowed to plant scary thoughts and then stand back and watch the bad guys turn white with fear as their imaginations run wild.

It doesn't take long to pry out the truth when you have two guys in separate rooms, each worried about being ratted out by the other. You get down to the nitty-gritty quickly.

Some of them will lawyer up. But a good lawyer knows that we are very skilled at flipping one bad guy on the other. If the attorney knows his client is not the actual shooter or is somehow less culpable than the other guy, he will offer to make a deal. Something along the lines of, "My client will offer a statement of what happened, in exchange for a plea deal . . ."

Then his client becomes your star witness after waiving his rights. You learn that there is no loyalty among murderers and thieves. They are street survivors, all about self-preservation. Most of them would roll over on their mother in a heartbeat if they thought it would keep them out of prison or off death row.

In this case, our friends Allan and Darnell quickly turned on each other like two tomcats eyeing the same tabby. Darnell came across as the more cooperative of the two. We voted him most likely to flip on his buddy.

Initially, he claimed to know nothing about the Elshire shooting. He said they had just been hanging out at his girlfriend's place before they ran into Ax and his handler.

"We saw the dog and got scared and ran," he said.

The kid had some skills as a liar.

We had more skills as truth-seekers.

We let him talk a bit, then took a break and sat down with his pal Al. We asked Lucero what he knew about the shooting, and he said, "Maybe I know who did it."

To which we responded, "What do you mean 'maybe'? If you know who did it, you'd better tell us right now."

It took him less than two seconds to throw his buddy under the bus. Lucero said Darnell shot and killed Mr. Elshire in a robbery attempt. Lucero claimed that he had watched the shooting from across the street. He noted that Darnell had carried three guns that night and dumped them as they left the scene.

We asked about the condom packages scattered everywhere. We had traced them to a nearby STD clinic run by the state department of health. They had bowls of condoms in the place to encourage people to avoid spreading sexually transmitted diseases.

Frick and Frack claimed they had found a big pile of them in the parking lot that night and stuffed them in their pockets. The condoms had fallen out during the robbery and while they were running away. We believed some of that story. A more likely scenario was that they planned on delivering the condoms to gang friends whose drug mules put narcotics in them, swallowed them, and transported them for distribution.

We wanted to know where the murder weapon and other guns had ended up, so we pressed Lucero to help us find them. We didn't tell him that we'd already found one, which wasn't the murder weapon. Lucero led us to the place where he said Darnell had thrown two more guns over the fence while fleeing the scene of the shooting.

We returned to our discussions with Darnell and fed him the news that his buddy was pointing the finger at him and had helped us recover two more guns, including the likely murder weapon.

"Your boy Allan gave you up," our detective told him.

Human nature being what it is, Darnell promptly flipped on Allan, claiming *he* did the shooting.

And so the dance continued.

One of our eyewitnesses had said she was fairly certain that the shooter wore gray pants. We had Darnell in a talkative mood, so we pushed him to describe what they each were wearing that night. He said Allan was wearing gray pants.

He also said they had changed clothes at the apartment where Darnell's girlfriend lived with her parents. We paid a visit to that apartment and found their clothing there. The girlfriend said Allan had worn the gray pants. In the pockets, we found shell casings and live .25-caliber rounds, which matched the murder weapon.

We took it all back to headquarters. We showed the pants to Allan Lucero, and he denied they were his. I threw them at him and told him to put them on. They fit perfectly.

Hey, it wasn't quite Cinderella and the glass slipper, but it worked for me. I was ready to put the squeeze on Allan Lucero to get his confession. We hadn't let him talk to his parents yet, but once we reached this stage, we brought them in because the law required their presence before we could get a signed statement.

The Luceros came. Both were in tears even though their son was still stone-faced and denying that he was the killer.

His parents urged him to tell the truth, which seemed to have very little impact on him.

We had an ace that we hadn't played, so we tossed it on the table.

"Allan, do you remember when you ran across the street that night and almost got hit by a car? Well, she saw your face, and she identified you as the shooter."

The kid was cornered, and he knew it. The presence of his parents made it unbearable.

"I shot him," he said.

He tried to justify it by saying he wanted money to help his parents pay the overdue rent.

Nice try, kid, but you don't get to take the life of a good man because you're trying to help out at home. He also claimed that Darnell had borrowed the guns, including the murder weapon, and had watched the whole thing go down.

Once a suspect has lied to me and I've called him out, he often will try to minimize or legitimize the crime or his involvement in it. Lucero claimed that Mr. Elshire took a swing at him. At one point, he even claimed the old guy pulled a knife. He was trying to justify shooting a guy who had just walked to the drugstore to get his wife some Rolaids.

With his sobbing parents beside him, our admitted killer said he had screamed "I'm sorry!" after shooting Robert Elshire. Then he ran, forgetting to take his victim's wallet.

He joined Darnell across the street, and they took off. They went to the apartment where Darnell's girlfriend lived with her parents. There, they changed clothes and hung out until they thought it would be safe to go back and get the borrowed guns.

That's when they got the Ax.

After we sorted out all their lies, we charged them both as adults for first-degree murder.

Two days after Dimond and Lucero were formally charged, the late Robert Elshire was honored by the participants in the Pikes Peak Ascent and Marathon, who wore patches on their arms in his memory.

TWISTED TRUTH

Since they were charged as adults, Allan Lucero and Darnell Dimond both received life sentences without parole. Unfortunately, Dimond had twisted the truth enough during our investigation to squirm his way out of prison after just six and a half years.

He initially told us he was eighteen years old, so we had refused to let his parents sit in on the first interrogation. Later, we learned that he was really seventeen, but we had already talked to him without his parents by then.

While in prison, he found a lawyer to challenge our case against him. In 2000, the Colorado Supreme Court ruled four to three that even though Dimond was interrogated as an adult because he had lied about his age, the statements he made during his interrogation should not have been admissible as evidence during his trial.

Apparently, four of the high-court dudes thought we should have time-traveled and fixed that, which is why I say you should never trust a man who wears a robe to work.

The Supremes did not set Dimond free, but they did say we would have to schedule a new criminal trial, in which we could not use much of the information from the first trial. The prospect of holding a second trial was further complicated by the fact that when this ruling came down, Dimond's partner in crime, Allan Lucero, was on the lam.

The admitted shooter in this case had decided to get out of prison, too, but he did it without a lawyer. Lucero and two other inmates climbed a twelve-foot fence topped with barbed wire, and absconded. Lucero was still AWOL when prosecutors were deliberating whether to retry Dimond. In the end, it was decided that we would have a hard time getting a conviction in a second trial, given the circumstances.

So the prosecutors offered Dimond a deal: plead guilty to a charge of serving as an accessory to murder, which was punishable by no more than six years in prison and three years parole.

Dimond, then twenty-three, took the deal and a get-out-of-jail-free card because he'd already served that time.

When this happened, Robert Elshire's family was disconcerted, to say the least, because Dimond served only six and a half years of a life sentence and Lucero was running free. Elshire's daughter, Connie Williams, made a good point. She told a local reporter, "The only person who got a long-term sentence out of this tragedy was my father."

Her anger and frustration were probably not all that soothed when Lucero was caught after twenty-four days on the run. They found him holed up in the Springs Motel, just a hundred yards from the central offices for the Colorado Department of Corrections.

At a press conference announcing Lucero's capture, a spokeswoman for the DOC noted that his hideout had been just across the parking lot. She said, "We have appreciated the irony."

Lucero was lucky they found him before I did.

And he was lucky that Ax had retired from the job.

CALLING OUT THE HOUNDS

Writing about my favorite four-legged crime-stopping companion called up memories of other K-9 unit members I worked with over the years. And since everyone loves a good dog story, I thought I'd share them with you.

If you are a cat person, just skip ahead to the next chapter.

We usually had twelve to sixteen canines with the department. Most of the time, they are in training or working. Theirs is not an easy life by any means, though they are very well cared for. Typically, these are Belgian Malinois or German shepherds, or a mix of those two breeds. These are not prissy purse puppies. They are large and intimidating beasts, for good reason.

The dogs and their handlers go through fifteen weeks of basic training, followed by six-to-eight weeks of field training, as well as four hours of ongoing training per week. Those dogs considered "dual purpose" get eight hours' training per week.

While K-9 units were first trained and deployed by law enforcement in Belgium in 1899, the first American city to train and use them was New York City, in 1911. Canines didn't come into widespread use by police departments across the USA until the 1950s.

They quickly proved themselves invaluable in our line of work. I checked recently, and my former department had eight patrol dogs, four bomb squad dogs, three airport security dogs, and one "undercover" dog assigned to assist the Metro Vice, Narcotics, and Intelligence divisions.

I had enormous respect and affection for our canines. I was very popular with them, perhaps because I kept a box of doggie-bone treats in my office. I was not above bribery, but only when it came to my furry friends.

This stash of treats resulted in one minor calamity thanks to a new K-9 recruit named Fonto, a German shepherd who was roughly the size of a Shetland pony. This dog was young, gangly, and not quite in full control of his massive body.

One day at police headquarters, Fonto's handler unleashed the dog, which was common on a quiet day. Fonto had already discovered my box of treats tucked in a corner, so he made a mad dash for my office.

I could hear him thundering down the hall and looked up to see Fonto flying toward my door. He made the ninety-degree turn—barely—but then went sliding and crashing into my file cabinet, knocking over the coffeemaker and a full pot on top of it. The broken glass and coffee sprayed across the room.

I jumped up to find Fonto staring at me while chomping on a treat. His look said, "Sorry, Lieutenant Kenda, I just couldn't help myself."

I forgave the dog immediately, but his handler had to buy me a new coffeepot.

We used our canines for a wide range of duties. They would help us search for suspects; find illegal drugs and weapons; hunt for cadavers; sniff out explosives; and intimidate, chase down, and subdue bad guys.

As most K-9 trainers will tell you, the dog's primary responsibility is to protect its handler and fellow officers, as well as the general public. They were formidable weapons when unleashed. They were not pets. We were never supposed to become too attached to our canines. In fact, if a K-9 handler became overly protective of his dog partner, he could be removed from the unit.

Our K-9 units were a critical tool in many of our investigations, and as one case in this book notes, they sometimes were the first to find the killer we were tracking, or the corpse or murder weapon we knew was out there.

For example, I had a case in which a woman heard some scratching at the front door of her home and found her live-in boyfriend sprawled on the porch, covered in blood from a gaping chest wound. He was alive, but he'd been severely stabbed.

When we asked where he'd been, she said, "He was playing poker with some friends in the neighborhood, but I don't know where they live."

Apparently, they played high-stakes poker. The game had turned ugly, and our victim got staked. We figured the boyfriend had crawled home before cashing in his chips, so to speak.

They shared a home in the middle of the city. We didn't know where he'd been, but we knew who could help us figure that out.

We called in the K-9 unit.

The handler arrived and put the dog on the scent. He took off down the street as if he knew where he was going. We followed man's best friend and tracker two blocks down and one block over. The dog then went up to the porch steps of a home and sat down, looking at us as if to say, "Well, I did my part. You boys take it from here!"

And we did. The dog had led us to the original scene of the assault, and that helped us identify the attacker and charge him. The stabber claimed self-defense, and the grand jury agreed with him.

THE BARK IS BAD, BUT THE BITE IS WORSE.

Each K-9 handler keeps his dog in the specially designed patrol car. If the officer gets out to make a traffic stop, he still has the power to release the dog remotely thanks to a control box worn on the uniform. If someone gives the officer a hard time, he or she can push a button that opens the door. The dog knows that this isn't a happy coincidence.

It comes to the officer's aid in a heartbeat. These are alpha dogs and extremely confrontational if need be. If you ever look at a police dog and it drops its head while maintaining eye contact, know that you have been put on notice. The dog is saying, "You wanna fuck with me or my handler, pal? Check out these teeth!"

The handler is required to give a warning before unleashing the K-9 weapon. If the dog is in its patrol car, the handler will issue the warning over the speakers mounted on the signal bar atop the roof. Those speakers are powerful and loud, so you can't ignore them. And you shouldn't!

Say, for example, a suspect is barricaded in a house. The K-9 handler will issue a warning like this: "Come out unarmed, with your hands visible. If you don't, we will release a police canine and enter the premises forcibly. Injury may result."

Now, the highly trained dog knows that this warning means "Game on." It is not an accident, then, that as the warning is being delivered, the dog goes absolutely bat-shit crazy, barking and growling in a roar that the speakers pick up and broadcast to the suspect.

This uproar makes the hound of the Baskervilles sound like Snoopy. The message is that this massive, muscular attack dog is ready and willing to tear into the flesh of the suspect unless compliance is forthcoming. In most cases, that message brings the desired result.

Another helpful hint about police dogs is that they are trained to respond to special commands delivered only in German, so yelling at them won't work. They won't listen to you. So you should comply before the dog is released.

The standard response is, "Okay, I'm coming out! Don't unleash that damned dog!"

This is because all humans share two instinctive fears embedded in our DNA. One is fire. The other is being devoured by a vicious beast. You can see these instincts kick in whenever you walk into a mob of people raising hell and then announce that you will be releasing your police dog unless they disperse peacefully.

One snarl from the canine usually does the trick. You can break up a mob of four hundred people in a couple of minutes. This also works well with suspects who are threatening to shoot us. We had a guy who didn't get the hint from the 150-pound German shepherd frothing at the mouth. He refused to drop his gun and surrender.

Instead, he turned and ran. The handler released his dog, and it was like a furred torpedo homing in on the target. Then he made the mistake of shooting at the dog. He missed. The dog did not.

They are trained to take away the weapon first. The canine slashed open the suspect's arm from elbow to wrist, forcing him to drop his gun. Then the dog went to work on the rest of him, sinking its teeth into his thigh. The shepherd's bite was so powerful that it crushed the guy's femur, the largest bone in the body.

After we subdued and arrested the screaming suspect, we took him to the emergency room. Doctors feared they might have to amputate his shattered leg, but instead they put a rod in it. The guy limped for the rest of his days, but it could have been worse. I'm certain he never ran from a police dog again, even if it were possible.

If you are contemplating resisting arrest in the future, please keep in mind that a K-9 handler generally can call off his unleashed beast if it is more than twenty feet from a suspect, but if the dog gets any closer, it is an uncontrollable, explosive, and potentially lethal weapon.

A trained attack dog can cause enormous harm and permanent injury, even death, in a matter of seconds. It will tear you limb from limb. We liked to say, "Every badass is a badass until a police canine tears into him. Then they squeal like little girls, screaming for help."

Bad persons with male parts might want to make a note to self: They will tear off your gonads and eat them. They might be less vicious with females, but I can't guarantee that.

As a detective, I used K-9 partners mostly for tracking and finding suspects, weapons, and victims. We once had a shooter at a city park who killed a woman and fled. Our police dog tracked the scent for a mile and a quarter, then stopped at a trash can and sat down. We opened it and found the shooter's clothing, which eventually led us to the killer.

K-9 units are remarkable. To help out a buddy, I actually had one live with me for six months. My friend had been a K-9 patrol officer and handler. He and his dog retired together, which is common. My buddy had to move into an apartment temporarily because he was building a new house and had sold his old one.

Most apartments will not take large German shepherds, even if they've retired from the police department. So I invited the dog, Harry Von Stroheim, to live with us. But only after my wife, Kathy, met with Harry and had a heart-to-heart about who really ran things.

Harry was intimidated, which proved once again how smart he was. So Harry moved in for six months. Now, at the time, we had a dog of our own, a chow chow named Simba. Despite the breed's silly name and fluffy, puffy, lionlike appearance, chows are very strong, quite protective, and can be aggressive.

Fortunately, Harry and Simba struck a truce early on. From the first day, they retired to opposite corners and rarely crossed paths. In truth, neither wanted to cross Kathy.

Harry lived with us back in the times when door-to-door salesmen were still common. Most of them were burglars casing out homes. A few of them actually sold magazines or spoiled meat products. Harry's handler told us that when a stranger came to the door, we should take the dog with us.

"If you get nervous about the person at the door, just reach down and pull up Harry's collar a half-inch or so. At that command, Harry will go into his bloodthirsty-werewolf routine, and your visitor will make a hasty departure."

Yes, we tried it. And yes, it worked.

Simba and Harry became a watchdog team. The shepherd watched the front door; the chow watched the back. We had no uninvited visitors drop by either entrance.

We did have one scary incident, though, when a team of carpet installers failed to heed our instructions and warnings about our canine corps. We put Harry and Simba in the kitchen, and Kathy had told the morons not to open any doors there while the workers were installing the new carpet.

"The dogs are aggressive, and we can't guarantee your safety if you open that door," my wife told them.

Well, they worked a while and got sweaty, so they opened the patio door, obviously forgetting about the dogs. Both Harry and Simba went out into the yard, scaring the shit out of the workers, who managed to flee. Simba stayed in the cul-de-sac in front of our house, but Harry decided to take a neighborhood tour.

When Kathy came home, Simba rose to greet her. She raised hell with the workers and asked where Harry had gone. They didn't know.

Kathy went looking for Harry. During her search, she flagged down a passing squad car, introduced herself as my wife, and commandeered it.

"You've got to help me find Harry," she said.

"Who's Harry?" they asked.

"One of your retired police dogs," she explained.

"Oh, shit," they both replied.

If a K-9-unit dog sees a police car, it will go to the car and climb into the back seat, so the patrol officers joined the search. They went one way; Kathy went the other.

She found Harry in a city park full of children. The mighty German shepherd was playing football with a bunch of little kids. The kids were chasing Harry and jumping on him, and he was loving it.

The unsuspecting parents were laughing and hugging the dog, too.

When Harry saw Kathy, his ears went down and his tail dropped between his legs.

"He's such a great dog," said one of the parents.

"Yes, he is, but Harry is a former police dog and he is AWOL, so I'm taking him home," said my wife.

The kids were not in danger, but if some adult had raised a hand to one of them or to Harry, carnage might have ensued.

Harry was a wonderful, smart dog. He responded to twenty-seven verbal commands and hand signals. He had assisted in more than fifty arrests in his long career. Kathy and I loved him, and when it came time for Harry to return to his handler, she tried to keep the dog and send me instead.

The handler was no dummy. He took Harry.

"Harry, let's go get some bad guys!"

The dog never looked back.

I told you Harry was smart.

CHAPTER TWO:
THE SERIAL KILLER NEXT DOOR

THE TRIGGER: SEXUAL RAGE

When my daughter, Kris, turned fifteen in 1986, she could shoot the eyes out of rattlesnake at fifty paces. A few years later, she scored 100 percent in her military shooting test.

When the instructor asked where she learned to shoot like that, she simply said, "My dad is a cop."

"No further explanation required," he said.

This was about the time Kris asked me when she could start dating.

"When you're sixteen," I said. "And when you turn twenty-eight, I might stop going with you."

Being a homicide detective can make you paranoid about protecting your family. Some say that paranoia is unreasonable, but not in my case. I had seen too many young women murdered by ruthless killers—some of whom the women had known and trusted.

That is one reason I asked my daughter to bring her male friends over so I could check them out. I did a rotten thing to my daughter one time. Her date came in this giant honking Buick station wagon, and he was so little, I couldn't see him behind the wheel when he pulled into our driveway.

I was home from work, but just for dinner, and I was still wearing my gun. I waited for him to walk up to the front door, and just as he was ringing the doorbell, I yanked the door open and said, "WHAT DO YOU WANT?"

I thought he had pissed his pants.

Kris didn't speak to me for two weeks. What can I say? I enjoyed playing the evil father. I trained both her and my son in firearms and self-defense because of disturbing cases like the one in this chapter, which I took more personally than most because it involved the murders of innocent young women like the one we were raising at the time.

Getting emotionally involved in my police work took a toll on me, as it does on every man and woman in law enforcement, whether they acknowledge it or not.

Yet, my empathy for victims also allowed me to hang on to my humanity. I have no regrets. Well, maybe in my darkest hours, I have some regrets. But my anger toward the killers, and my determination to seek justice made me push myself and my team all the harder.

That was the case with Micki Filmore, whose life ended at the age of twenty-two. This country girl from rural North Carolina had joined the army straight out of high school. She did a three-year tour of duty and saw a lot of the world before her service ended in December 1985.

Sadly, I was called to her one-bedroom in Pikes Peak Apartments seven months later, on July 19, 1986. One of her neighbors, Army Specialist Tracy Spencer, called us to say he'd walked by her apartment window and seen Micki sprawled on the floor. She didn't move when he knocked on the window.

Spencer and his wife had seen their neighbor having pizza the night before. They said she had seemed fine then, so this alarmed him. He went back to his apartment and told his wife, Lisa.

They returned, and Spencer helped his wife climb through an open window of the apartment to check on Micki. They found a disturbing scene. She was dead and sprawled naked after an apparent sexual assault.

Our homicide unit was called to the apartment shortly thereafter, and we found the scene no less disturbing. The victim was on the floor with her legs apart. We wondered whether the killer had positioned her this way for a purpose.

She also had bruising around her neck, suggesting that she'd been raped and strangled. Nothing in the apartment appeared to be disturbed, raising the distinct possibility that rape and murder, not burglary, had been the killer's goal.

There was no sign of forced entry, which also raised questions. Micki Filmore may have left her door unlocked, which seemed unlikely for a woman who had traveled the world through her military service.

The killer may have entered through the same unlocked window that the Spencers had used. Or, more likely, Micki may have known her killer and trusted him enough to let him in.

There was something particularly twisted in this case, and as the father of a young daughter, I left the murder scene with my stomach in knots. My sense was that we were dealing with a deranged and calculating killer.

I feared that unless we found this person soon, he would strike again. My fear was not misplaced.

A GREATER SENSE OF URGENCY

I always carried a sense of urgency into murder investigations. A killer was on the loose, after all. But I didn't always have the sense of dread that came with this one. Part of it, I'm sure, was paternal. My young daughter lived in this city, too. Yet that didn't explain the nagging sense that this was someone who was not done killing.

He had selected his victim, stalked her, and struck swiftly and viciously. I had the definite impression that he was a compulsive killer, who would not be satiated and, in fact, was probably already searching for his next victim.

I called in all available officers and detectives to interview residents of the apartment complex, which had a large contingent of military and former-military personnel. Colorado Springs had more than forty thousand military personnel assigned to five military bases in our area. Most were good citizens, but when you have a large group of individuals who have worked in violent environments and have access to firearms, there will always be a percentage who cause problems in the community.

We always had a very good relationship with the military police, who handled crimes on their bases while we handled those within our jurisdictions. We often socialized, as well as worked together on cases that crossed jurisdictional lines. The military's Criminal Investigations Division (CID) team wore civilian clothes and carried the title "agent" rather than military rankings.

In recent years, the two separate law enforcement agencies worked together to solve a cold case dating back to my years with the Colorado Springs Police Department. This was a 1987 case of mine, which was similar to the Filmore murder. An active-duty soldier stationed at Fort Carson, Darlene Krashoc, twenty, was raped and murdered. Our patrol officers found her behind a Korean restaurant in the city on March 17.

She was last seen alive between midnight and one a.m., a mile from the restaurant, at a nightclub called Shuffles, where she was drinking and dancing with other soldiers. She'd been beaten and strangled, and it appeared that her body had been moved to the restaurant parking lot after she was killed.

We worked the investigation with the support of the CID agents from Fort Carson. Together, we collected evidence and interviewed witnesses, but we could never nail down a suspect, I'm afraid.

Eventually, her murder investigation was assigned to a cold case unit. Over the years, they reviewed it, and as the science of DNA testing and analysis improved, they kept on top of it to see how it might be applied in the Krashoc case.

In 2016, investigators in the CSPD cold case unit, which I created, even hired a private company that uses state-of-the-art technology to predict the physical appearance and ancestry of suspects based on DNA phenotyping. Once they had a composite sketch, the army offered a ten-thousand-dollar reward for information that would lead them to Krashoc's killer.

We all hoped that move would at least bring some leads, but again, nothing of value turned up. Then the cold case guys took another look at what they might do with the DNA evidence taken from the crime scene more than thirty years earlier.

They had learned about a new investigative tool after hearing that police in California had finally made an arrest in the infamous "Golden State killer" case in 2018. This involved a serial killer believed to have murdered at least a dozen people and raped at least forty-five women in California from 1976 to 1986.

The California investigators had gathered DNA evidence, but they never found a match in the standard law enforcement databases. The break in their case came when a detective decided to compare that DNA with a more recently created database. This one contained DNA voluntarily submitted by the millions of people eager to learn more about their heritage and track their relatives and ancestors through services like Ancestry. com and FamilyTreeDNA.

The California detectives found a lead at GEDmatch, a free service that had been used by a relative of the man they eventually arrested, Joseph James DeAngelo, a seventy-two-year-old former police officer who had lived in the area where victims were found.

When the relative's DNA matched that of the suspected serial killer, it put the detectives on his trail because it had to be someone in that immediate family. They then tracked down DeAngelo and charged him.

Even while that case was awaiting trial, law enforcement agencies from all over the country began following the same procedure, submitting DNA from their cold cases to the genetic-testing databases. The investigators in the Krashoc case tried it. They found matches that led them to Michael Whyte, a nineteen-year army veteran who had been stationed at Fort Carson and lived just three blocks from where Darlene's body was found.

He had married, gone on to have a long career as a network engineer, and had no criminal record. Our guys worked with the army investigators to gather information and put Whyte under surveillance. The plan was to somehow secure some of his DNA and compare it directly to that gathered in the Krashoc case.

They followed him one day to a Starbucks, where he ordered a cup of coffee, sat down and drank it, and then discarded the paper cup in the trash. As soon as he walked out the door, our guys ran in and grabbed the cardboard cup and took his DNA sample from it. The lab results came back as a match, so they obtained a warrant and arrested him on charges of first-degree murder and aggravated sexual assault.

This trial is still pending as of this publication.

Since the Micki Filmore murder occurred in an apartment complex that was not on military property, my division handled the investigation, but we always knew we could count on the military investigators to help us with any information or backup we needed from them.

WADING THROUGH THE LIKELY SUSPECTS

In our talks with Filmore's neighbors, we learned that Micki had recently split with a fiancé and was having financial problems. One neighbor, Jesse Capparelli, whose unit was next to the victim's, knew her well and offered a story that immediately snared our attention.

He told us he'd been to a nightclub with her on the night of her death, though they were not dating or involved. Capparelli said that during their visit to the club, another man approached Filmore. She appeared to know him. They talked like friends. The neighbor saw her give that man a piece of paper.

The neighbor said he and Micki returned to their complex at about two a.m., talked briefly, and then went to their respective apartments. But then, about 3:45 a.m., he heard someone knocking on Micki's door. Capparelli looked out and saw the man whom Filmore had talked to in the club. So he went back to bed, figuring Micki had invited him over.

Another neighbor, Frances Stanford, told our guys that she'd heard a loud scream and a thumping sound come from Filmore's apartment around the same time. She assumed there was a fight underway, and went back to bed. It would be a long time before anyone in that apartment complex ever again ignored strange noises in the night.

The autopsy on Micki Filmore cleared up a few things. She wasn't intoxicated at the time of her death. Nor was she pregnant, although we'd heard a report to the contrary. We had also been told that she'd recently broken up with her fiancé. We contacted him and learned that he was actually finalizing a divorce so he could marry Micki. He also had an alibi for the time of her murder.

The fiancé told us he had asked a Colorado Springs friend, Doug Barth, to look after Micki while he was gone. When he learned of her death, he expressed concerns that maybe his friend was involved in it.

This made me wonder at the quality of his friendships, but we went a-hunting for Mr. Barth and found him. He had an alibi for the night of the murder, so we put him on the back burner. We'd found a more likely suspect by that time, anyway.

Our detectives had turned up the name of Karl Cloves as the man who had talked with Micki in the nightclub, received a piece of paper from her, and then went knocking on her door in the middle of the night.

We tracked him down, and Cloves admitted that he had run into Micki at the club, danced with her, and asked for her phone number after she assured him that the neighbor with her was not a suitor.

Being part man and part hound dog, Cloves assumed that meant she was okay with him coming to her apartment at 3:45 a.m. He claimed that he knocked, but she didn't answer. Using his keen powers of deduction, he figured she may have fallen asleep, so he left.

"I did see that her neighbor friend was checking out his window to see who was at Micki's door," he added. "But I didn't stick around to talk to him, or anything."

Naturally, we didn't take his word for that. When he had trouble accounting for his whereabouts the rest of the night, we decided to keep him under lock and key. Cloves's behavior didn't help him. Aside from being arrogant, he seemed not to care that this young woman had been murdered.

We asked for some samples of body fluid and he complied. It always takes a few weeks to get the results, and if he was the killer, I wanted him off the street.

UPPING THE ANTE

Three weeks into this investigation we had identified a couple of solid suspects, but we hadn't been able to nail anyone down for certain, which was beyond frustrating. We still were very interested in Karl Cloves and preparing to dig deeper into his background, when my worst fear came true.

On August 12, there was another murder in the Pikes Peak Apartments complex. And it was another young woman. Right under our noses.

You can imagine my rage.

No, you probably can't.

This case was already personal for me because of the first young female victim and what was done to her. Now it was threatening my reputation and my career. I had no doubt it was the same killer, and he had thrown down the gauntlet.

The second victim was Barbara Kramer, twenty-four, a nurse at Eisenhower Hospital. My wife was a nurse at a different hospital, so that poured even more salt into the wound.

When Barbara Kramer didn't show up for work, the hospital tried to reach her and couldn't, so they contacted her sister. She found yesterday's newspaper sitting outside the door of the apartment. This was not a good sign.

Barbara Kramer's sister and other family members had talked to her about the previous murder in her apartment complex. They had offered to let her stay with them, but she assured everyone that she would be extra careful.

If that was the case, her killer must have been particularly cunning.

They found her body in her apartment bedroom. A few pieces of furniture were moved or overturned. There were few other signs of a struggle.

Her family was devastated, and very angry with the Colorado Springs Police Department and its homicide unit. I couldn't blame them. I was equally pissed off—maybe more so, because after seeing the crime scene, I knew that it had to be the same guy.

He'd picked a similar target: a young woman living alone. He left Barbara Kramer in much the same position as he'd left Micki Filmore. Both victims were attacked between four a.m. and seven a.m., raped, and strangled.

With the first case, we had considered that Filmore's death might have resulted from accidental strangulation as the result of rough or "edge" sex, in which one partner chokes the other. When this crime occurred, in the late 1980s, this sort of thing was mostly limited to couples who were into sexual bondage and dominance role-playing.

We didn't see a lot of deaths related to it back then, but with the spread of internet porn over the past several decades, there have been a lot more cases of sex-related deaths through accidental strangulation.

I advise anyone who has teenagers, male or female, to discuss the dangers of this sort of sex. One study found that nearly a quarter of adult women in the United States have felt scared during sex, and one of the reasons is because partners tried to choke them, thinking it was an okay thing to do. It's not. Even if both people have talked about it and agreed to this form of sex, there is a very real danger that you can be seriously injured or killed.

We considered that this might have happened to Micki Filmore, but when the second victim was also strangled after being raped, it pretty much eliminated that theory. These killings appeared to be intentional and planned out.

We were looking at a potential serial killer targeting young women in our city, and that was a chilling thought for everyone. Nothing gets the media more churned up, and city officials more outraged, than a serial killer on the loose.

As head of our homicide unit, I was up against the wall. Especially since this second attack obviously eliminated one of our top suspects, Cloves, the guy who had met Filmore at the bar and then gone to her apartment. We had to let him go, which meant our killer was still out there, unafraid and on the prowl.

After studying this second crime scene, I went outside and stood on the second-floor balcony of the apartment building, looking into the central courtyard. I was so despondent and mortified that I actually considered throwing myself off.

The only thing that stopped me was that two stories wasn't all that high, and I didn't want to end up both paralyzed and pissed off.

The pressure was intense. The press targeted me, which came with the job, so I was the subject of the dreaded "POLICE BAFFLED" headlines. My bosses felt free to blame me for the killer remaining on the loose. My own guys hated me because I was working them like dogs.

So I was universally despised outside my immediate family, and Kathy wasn't all that happy with me either, because I was either gone all the time or home being a sullen SOB.

I was obsessed with finding this killer, who definitely had a modus operandi. This was not a simple home invasion or crime of opportunity. There did not appear to be any search for money, drugs, or guns.

There was no ransacking, no sign of extended fighting, very little out of place in either apartment. The disturbed areas were very limited. Once he was in the door, he appeared to overwhelm his victims quickly and then rape them.

He got in and out fast, and there appeared to be no forcible entry. This indicated that his victims knew him or might at least recognize him. That led me to believe that he lived in the same apartment complex. He gained entrance because his victims knew him, and he didn't stick around, for fear of being recognized by other residents.

This was a large apartment complex with people working different shifts, coming and going and hanging out twenty-four hours a day. Many of the doorways were easily visible to other tenants. I figured that was why he wanted to get in and out fast.

And if he lived there, it was easy for him to stalk his neighbors and make them his victims. This was all just conjecture on my part, but it made sense based on the evidence.

He was looking like a serial killer. They were usually cunning, but their bloodlust often led them to take greater and greater risks, which eventually led to mistakes. Sooner or later, someone would spot him and remember.

Then it would be *our* turn to pounce.

The sooner, the better.

NEIGHBORHOOD WATCH

Panicking and blaming don't solve homicide cases. Good old-fashioned police work often does, and in this case, our nonstop interviews with residents of the Pikes Peak Apartment complex eventually paid off with a major break in the case.

One resident reported hearing screams from Barbara Kramer's apartment sometime after six a.m. That was only of marginal help, but it allowed us to nail down the time frame.

And then another resident helped us home in on a suspect. This neighbor looked out a window around the same time and saw none other than Tracy Spencer banging on Kramer's door, while holding a piece of paper in his hand, around 6:25 a.m.

Spencer had claimed he discovered Micki Filmore's body while walking by her apartment window. And now we had a witness who saw him knocking on the second victim's door around the time she'd been murdered?

Well, isn't that interesting!

We had already looked into Spencer's criminal history. He had some minor offenses, though nothing to suggest that he might be a serial rapist and killer. Even so, his presence was confirmed at both crime scenes around the time the rapes and murders occurred, and that was enough to secure an arrest warrant.

The bosses were pressuring me to go for it, but I wanted to make one more run at his wife, Lisa. I wanted to see if she was still standing by the story that she'd been the first to go inside Micki Filmore's apartment after her husband spotted her body through a window.

She had been fairly convincing when we first talked to her, but I wondered how she would respond if we turned up the heat a little. Why would any woman protect a man who was raping and killing other women? Maybe she feared him. That would certainly be understandable. But what if we promised to put him away for the rest of his life? Would she still protect the asshole then?

SPOUSAL ABUSE

Two of our ace interrogators—excuse me, *interviewers*—sat down with Lisa Spencer and gently but firmly put her through the meat grinder.

No, I jest. They went at her lightly, knowing that she might well be terrified of her husband.

They promised to protect her and told her that we needed to stop this
killer, whoever he was, before he claimed more victims.

"Lisa, was Tracy really with you every moment on the night of Micki
Filmore's killing, before the discovery of her body? Or had he gone out
earlier?"

She tried to stick with the lie, briefly, but when they told her a witness
had seen her husband outside Barbara Kramer's apartment on the night
of her murder—making him the only person to be seen at both apartments on the nights of the murders—Lisa's carefully constructed story
began to fall apart.

"He went out for a walk earlier. He always goes out for walks at night,
leaving me for hours," she said. "He never tells me where he goes."

"Do you think he's meeting other women?"

"I don't know," she said. "I wouldn't be all that surprised. He's aggressive that way. He likes it rough."

We found that interesting, too.

Then Lisa Spencer gave us another nail for her husband's coffin.

On the night of Barbara Kramer's death, her husband told her that
he'd found some of Kramer's mail on the ground near the apartment
complex mailboxes and wanted to return it to her.

"I'd already found an empty stamped envelope with her name on it,
but I didn't tell him that. I just threw it away," she said. "He was really
mad when he couldn't find it."

That explained why these women opened the door for him—he was
pretending to have pieces of their mail that he'd found.

Our detectives then asked Lisa if she had really gone to Micki Filmore's apartment after her husband claimed he'd seen her lying on the floor.

"No, he made me do that to help him create a cover story," she said.

"Why would you do that?" our guy asked. "Why would you help him
cover up something so terrible as that?"

"I loved him," she said.

I knew love was blind, but I didn't think it was that stupid.

ONE GOOD LIE DESERVES ANOTHER

As our detectives were loading up on damning testimony against Tracy Spencer, we learned that he might be planning to flee the area, so we got our warrant and snatched him up without a fight.

We searched the house and found the envelope with Barbara Kramer's name on it in the trash, where Lisa Spencer had said she put it.

I questioned Tracy Spencer after telling him we were charging him with both murders. He stuck to his story for the most part, though he did admit to taking a piece of Barbara Kramer's mail to her that night.

"But I never went inside," he said.

It was obvious that this guy was a pathological liar, so I decided to try out one of my own.

"You know, we took samples from Micki Filmore's body, and you were a match," I said.

"Yeah, well, that's because we'd been having an affair, but I didn't kill her," he said. "She was into me."

This guy had a bullshit answer for everything, but we had him by the gonads at that point. When the lab results did come back, his blood and hair samples matched those found at both crime scenes.

We had also turned up other damning evidence once we had Spencer locked up. While searching his apartment, we found a necklace that had belonged to one of his victims. Some serial killers have been known to keep mementos from their victims, though I wouldn't say it's all that common. It is, however, very common for child molesters to stockpile them. We always look for them and nearly always find them hidden away somewhere in their homes or cars or storage lockers.

During our search of Spencer's home, we also found a bizarre series of notes that he appeared to have written to himself. In one of them, he wrote something along the lines of, "I'm sorry I do bad things." It wasn't exactly a confession note—more a general statement of regret.

It's hard to say what went on in this guy's head. He was a strange one. He didn't fit any mold even though the two murders we nailed him for were very similar. While looking into his past, we discovered that he had also killed an elderly woman when he was a juvenile, in an attempted robbery.

The victim was in her eighties, and she died after Spencer knocked her down in the robbery. This had occurred in Mississippi and was in juvenile records there, which is why we didn't find it earlier in our investigation. He was found guilty and served prison time, but apparently, he wasn't in for long.

We couldn't use the juvenile record against him, but even so, we had enough evidence that Spencer pleaded guilty on December 31, 1986, to one count of first-degree murder and one count of second-degree murder for the deaths of two women, in exchange for withdrawal of the death penalty.

The court sentenced him to life imprisonment on the first-degree murder count and twenty-four years in prison on the second-degree murder count, with the sentences to be served consecutively. The goal was to make sure he stayed behind bars for the rest of his life, and as far as I know, he is still locked up.

RARE BEAST

Our killer in this case was a rare beast: an instinctive bad guy—one of the few I ran across in my many years of locking up shitheads, male and female. He killed at least twice, and the second time was right under our noses. Both victims were raped, although the earlier case in his juvenile records was a robbery gone wrong.

Sex was a trigger in our two cases, and it's a wild card in any murder investigation. A psychiatrist once told me that he'd be willing to spend hours discussing homicidal triggers with me, unless sex was involved.

"If these murders are sex-related, all bets are off," he said. "You cannot predict behaviors that involve sexual urges and desires. After the survival instinct, our sexual instincts are the most powerful driving force in human behavior."

If someone's sex drive is twisted beyond what society considers normal or legal or safe, there is no way to correct the resulting behavior, he said. "It's too strong a drive." That's why most psychiatrists will tell you that child molesters cannot be "cured" or successfully treated.

My own experience in dealing with sex-related crimes, including homicide, is that there are no limits to the depravity of humans. Tracy Spencer probably didn't understand what drove him to kill these two women. His wife said he was into rough sex, but he hadn't killed her. So why did he kill our two victims? We will likely never know. He was a very strange beast.

We were haunted by the thought that this demon may well have killed others before we found his trail. We did find it unusual that he was married, given his apparent hatred of women. A psychiatrist might have been able to figure out his wife's loyalty and love for him; it remains beyond my comprehension. During interviews, he was difficult to read. His emotions were all over the place. One minute, he'd be tearfully protesting his innocence, and then a switch would flip, and he would become very cold and disconnected.

His behavior was often bizarre. He'd surge with energy that had him bouncing his knees, wriggling in his chair, and wringing his hands, and then he'd get nearly comatose. During one interview, Spencer claimed he was affected by "lunar cycles," as if he were a werewolf or vampire.

There are many varying opinions on the influence of the moon's phases on human behavior. Some scientists say it's more myth than fact. Most cops and ER doctors will tell you that things get very busy for them when there is a full moon.

But lunar cycles are no excuse for the sort of lunacy perpetrated by Tracy Spencer. I have no doubt that he would have killed more women had we not stopped him. So, yes, I believe he was a serial killer. He was bent on punishing women. It was not about sexual gratification. It was about hurting other humans.

Needless to say, he was a sick son of a bitch. When he picked up his mail, he'd steal letters addressed to women he targeted, and use that to get them to open their doors.

He went out at night to choose those victims; then he'd watch and observe them, like a wolf selecting its prey. He took his time and selected the most vulnerable women. He had malice aforethought, as the lawyers say, and that made him particularly dangerous.

He would overpower them quickly, rape them, and then strangle them. Choking someone to death is an act of pure hatred. Studies have found that it is the method used in about 35 percent of serial murders. Those killers are more likely to choke victims to death than are those who kill only one person. Psychiatrists believe that those who kill repeatedly use strangulation because they feel more powerful and in control than they would using a weapon.

Rapists don't often kill their victims unless it's accidental. They usually want them to suffer for a long time after the actual attack, because rape is driven more by a twisted hatred of women.

We once had a serial rapist in Colorado Springs who attacked nearly forty women, but he did not kill any of them even though he threatened them with a knife. Then again, there are always exceptions. Humans are complicated, and violent criminals are even more so. The experts will tell you also that it is rare for a rapist to attack women of different races.

Yet Micki Filmore was Black, and Barbara Kramer was white.

We didn't just shut the book on this case after Spencer was locked up. We put a lot of time into looking for similar cases of rape and murder in our region and around the country, but we couldn't connect Tracy Spencer to any of them.

I still wonder if there were others out there. He killed at least three times, and the third was right under our noses. That didn't sit well.

I have no doubt that Spencer would have killed more women had we not stopped him. He had no fear of law enforcement. In his mind, we did not matter. All that mattered to him was raping and killing.

Well, we took that away from him. So I guess we do matter after all.

WHICH REMINDS ME . . .

Writing about the Tracy Spencer homicides took me back to my nine months as watch commander for the Colorado Springs Police Department's Sand Creek substation. I had been promoted from detective sergeant to lieutenant. The plan was for me to do a tour of other divisions before taking over as head of Homicide.

Sand Creek was our busiest substation. From there, we ran patrols in the neighborhood that included Spencer's apartment building, where his victims also lived, as well as all the subsidized apartment projects in the city—in general, a low-income population.

The Sand Creek substation was known by everyone in the police department as "Fort Apache" in reference to the 1981 movie *Fort Apache, The Bronx*, starring Paul Newman as a veteran cop in a crime-ridden precinct of New York City. For my tour, I was the watch commander for the "cocktail shift" there, between two p.m. and ten p.m. Those were wild times.

When word got out that there was a tough new sheriff in town, the negative reaction wasn't limited to local outlaws. On my first day, I made an inspection of our small building. I wandered back into the locker room used by the male patrol officers to change into and out of their uniforms.

Two young cops were in there. They couldn't see me as I approached on the other side of the lockers, but I could hear them talking.

"Who's the new commander?" asked one.

"Lieutenant Kenda," said the other.

"You mean the *murder guy*? I heard he's a fucking monster!"

"Jesus, I've heard the same thing about him."

I was enjoying their banter but decided to stick my head around the corner and interrupt.

"Boys, the monster will see you in lineup in five minutes."

Those two patrol officers worked hard to avoid me for the next six months.

I have to admit, that was a fun tour of duty for me because it was the Wild West and I was the sheriff. In just one week, we had more than a hundred reports of shots fired along one street in our patrol area. Residents were terrified, and my phone was ringing off the hook.

Finally, I rounded up twenty police cruisers and the officers to drive them, and we did a convoy with lights flashing and sirens screaming up and down that street. Then, once everyone was out on the porches and lawns, I got on my vehicle's public address system and put out a message:

"We are tired of coming down here every five minutes, so if you all don't stop fighting and shooting, I'm locking down this neighborhood. You won't be

able to jaywalk, spit on the sidewalk, drop a piece of paper, or drive more than a block in your car without being stopped, questioned, and maybe even given a citation or thrown in jail."

Basically, I was telling them that the neighborhood better quiet down or we were going to be up their asses 24-7 until it did. The hard-ass tactics worked. I learned that the residents appreciated a strong police presence.

A sense of humor helped, too.

One night at Sand Creek, two patrol officers yelled for me to come back into our holding cell. I hustled back there and found them struggling with a big guy they'd arrested. He was fighting with them, bouncing all over the room and getting in some good licks.

I said, "Why don't you just settle down before I call in a whole bunch of badass cops who will beat you into submission? You can't win this battle. We will outnumber you, and the only possible result is that you will get beat up and still be in jail facing even more charges."

He glared at me, unimpressed with my reasoning.

"Fuck off, you white saltine-cracker motherfucker," he said.

"Hey, that's *Lieutenant* White Saltine-Cracker Motherfucker to you!"

He stopped fighting because he was laughing so hard, and as he sat down and let them cuff him, he looked at me and said, "Ha! You are all right, man!"

I felt a connection to the neighborhood even though I didn't look like most of its residents. I'd come up in a hardscrabble place, too, but this was a much tougher, poorer area—and especially hard on the children.

One of my most unpleasant duties was to supervise a mass court-ordered "children exchange" every other weekend in the parking lot of our substation. This was where divorced couples who had visitation rights on alternating weekends would bring their kids to switch sides for the weekend.

A judge had ordered this potentially volatile exchange to be done at the police substation to cut down on the hostilities between ex-spouses that often occurred in these situations.

Eleven families had been ordered to participate.

Imagine dozens of little kids crying and dragging their suitcases— usually little more than plastic bags—across the parking lot as their warring parents glared and shouted insults at each other.

None of my patrol officers wanted to supervise this, because it was such a volatile and heartbreaking event. So I usually just did it myself, and then I went home and hugged my kids, probably for longer than they wanted.

Along with overseeing that horrendous undertaking and commanding the patrol officers cruising the area, I had to handle any civilians who stumbled in with complaints, tips, or lunatic demands.

There wasn't much staff in the office, because our patrol officers were always on the street. My first line of defense was Frannie. She was a police service representative. She was not a cop. She was more of a traffic controller. She decided what to do with walk-ins, whether to chase them out or let them talk to me.

One night, poor Frannie had about fifteen people lined up waiting to be screened. She was trying to keep them away from me because I had an important visitor, a two-star general who had just taken command of the Fourth Infantry Division at Fort Carson.

Since a lot of his military personnel lived off base in our neighborhood, he had come in to meet me and to do a ride along with our patrol officers. He wanted to get a feel for the area and the living environment. I was glad that he'd shown such an interest.

At the same time, I had another visitor, who wasn't all that welcome in my office. She was a large and belligerent juvenile who'd been taken into custody. She was sitting in my office only because we didn't have any other place to put her due to overcrowding and her female juvenile status.

She was supposed to sit there and keep her mouth shut while I talked to my more dignified high-ranking guest. Instead, she kept calling me and everyone else "motherfucker."

This did not sit well with the general, as you might expect.

While I was worrying about the possibility of a brawl between the military leader and the juvenile street thug in my office, Frannie came barging in and said, "There is a man out front who says he has a bomb in his shopping bag."

It was going to be that kind of night at Fort Apache.

I flew out the door, telling the female juvenile to stay put but letting the general make his own decision.

There, in our small waiting area, stood a man with a paper bag that had smoke coming out of it. Not a lot of smoke, but smoke.

"I think it's some sort of explosive device," he said. "It was already smoking when I found it."

"Where did it come from?" I asked while ushering him and his bag out into the parking lot.

"Well, you see, I'm banging this broad who is married, but I didn't know that. Apparently, her husband found out. He's an army guy, and I think he tried to blow up my car with this, but I think the fuse went out or it fizzled."

"Call the bomb squad," I told Frannie.

The general had wandered out and heard the explanation. As we walked back into my office, he shook his head and told me, "You know, I served in Desert Storm and I never encountered anything like this place."

"Fuck you!" said my other visitor.

"Yeah, we're having a real Fort Apache night," I told the general.

There were a lot of murders in the Sand Creek substation's patrol area, and a high percentage of them occurred in the vicinity of a large nightclub called La Jazz Affaire. In one year alone, we had more than a hundred calls to the club and its parking lot.

From time to time, because of the club's reputation for violence, the military would ban any of its members from going there. After we had six homicides in or around the jazz club within three weeks, a community meeting was called.

I wasn't surprised when residents and business owners in that area invited me to attend. I was surprised, however, that the event was being held inside La Jazz Affaire and hosted by its notorious owner, Charles Collins.

Collins was a slick and clever fellow. He tended toward flashy suits and Dobermans with spiked collars and rarely ventured out without the company of two large fellows, also in suits, whom he claimed were his lawyers.

I went to the meeting with my division commander, Captain O, and we were amused to find they were serving wine, cheese, and other foods. We ordered soft drinks, of course.

"This is going to be interesting," said my commander.

This was in a predominantly Black neighborhood, so Captain O and I were the only two white people present. There was also one prominent Korean businesswoman there, wearing a miniskirt, six-inch heels, and a look of contempt.

Her name sounded like "Son Okay," and she owned a restaurant and bar next door. We knew the place because neighbors were always complaining about the smell from it.

Also, she'd had a homicide in her own parking lot recently. Son Okay was not okay with all the crime and its impact on her bottom line.

Despite some tensions in the room, the midday meeting started out very cordial and polite. Most people were drinking wine and booze. Once everyone settled in, Collins, with his Dobermans at his side, stood up, introduced himself, and launched into a very heartfelt speech.

He reminded me of a preacher, and a very smooth one at that.

"We are all gathered here in company of our local police department to discuss a terrible wave of criminal activity. We are concerned business leaders, taxpayers, and citizens, and today we'd like to hear everyone's thoughts on what is causing this problem in our community."

Just then Son Okay raised her hand like a kid in class and shouted out in broken English, "The problem is, there are too many damned (racial epithet) in this neighborhood!"

This particular racially charged word is considered a fighting word, like yelling "fire" in a crowded theater—only worse in this situation.

The previously cordial crowd instantly turned into a very angry mob. Threats and curses spewed. A large fellow seated next to Son Okay rose from his chair and loomed over her, making threats.

She whipped off a six-inch heel and smacked him in the nose with the spiked end. He went facedown in his cheese plate, out cold in his Colby and crackers.

The place went up for grabs. The Dobermans were barking and snarling. Son Okay went into full ninja mode, dropping people left and right with her stilettos until someone whacked her with a chair and knocked her into us.

Captain O and I were a little slow in taking command of the situation anyway. We couldn't get up, because we were laughing so hard at the sight of this tiny Asian woman whipping up on everyone around her.

Finally, we got to our feet, radioed for assistance, and settled everyone down. We arrested eight people at the community meeting called to restore peace and order to the neighborhood.

Such was life at Fort Apache in the Wild West of Colorado Springs.

CHAPTER THREE:
THE COMING UNDONE OF A GOOD MAN

THE TRIGGER: DEMENTIA

The human mind is an immensely complicated piece of machinery. Nobody knows how it works and why people do what they do. If I did, I'd write a psychological bestseller, retire, and move to the south of France.

I am not a psychologist or psychiatrist, but I have been a witness to every bizarre behavior you can imagine. I can tell you from a wealth of haunting experience that there is no limit to the level of violence or depravity in humans.

I saw it day in and day out. Even so, this case was a startling event that stands out in my memories after a long career working deep in the mines of madness.

A .357 Magnum is incredibly loud. When fired, the sound is like that of a field howitzer. The explosion reverberates and echoes for miles. On this occasion, around eight a.m. on August 20, 1987, the blast triggered 911 calls from a wide radius on the north side of the city of Colorado Springs.

Everyone heard something, but no one saw a thing; except for one caller who had heard a woman shout, "What do you want from me!" The caller then looked out a window and saw a man and the victim arguing. Seconds later, she heard a loud gunshot and saw a young woman on the ground, with blood spewing from her head.

She then called our department. Our 911 operators dispatched all available units to a well-kept 1940s-era one-story apartment complex that had rarely been the scene of a crime.

Except on this day, when it was the scene of a slaughter.

Our officers arrived and found a female victim in the parking lot near a maroon Pontiac Grand Am parked in a spot reserved for guests of the apartment residents. She had been shot in the head at close range. Lucinda "Linde" Moore, thirty, was still hanging on to life, but barely. She died shortly after arriving at the hospital.

Linde Moore would prove to be only the first of far too many victims in this bizarre and tragic case.

I was at police headquarters, meeting with detectives about another murder case, when the call came on a possible fatal shooting in a north-side apartment complex. A quiet morning suddenly became very busy.

Our officers were interviewing neighbors when we arrived. They filled me in. Upon arriving, they learned from one neighbor that the victim was the daughter of residents Hank and Ola Mae Waller, who managed the apartment complex.

This witness, Sarah Spann, had been our 911 caller. She had identified the man she saw arguing with the victim as Linde's father. Ms. Spann said that Linde, a registered nurse, sometimes dropped off her son to stay with his grandparents while she went to work at St. Francis Hospital.

Mrs. Spann provided their apartment number to our first guys there. Our officers had found a rear door unlocked, announced their presence, and entered with guns drawn. They were aware that a shooter might be inside.

They found a kitchen table set for a family breakfast that had not happened and never would. Glasses were full of orange juice, but no one was there. No sights or sounds of activity.

Our guys had moved through the apartment cautiously, prepared to shoot as they opened closet doors and checked rooms. Down a hallway, they found the master bedroom—and a heartbreaking, deeply disturbing scene.

In that moment and many times afterward when my mind flashed back to that case, I asked myself, *Why do I do this for a living?*

Hank Waller, fifty-six, was on the floor, dead from what appeared to be a close-range gunshot to the head. Our officers earlier found a male child in his arms, as if he'd had the boy in a headlock. The child had also been shot in the head at close range. The first responders found him still breathing, so they had taken him to the hospital.

We would learn later that this was Waller's seven-year-old grandson, Brandon Moore, whose mother, Linde, had been found in the parking lot. The boy died shortly after arriving at the hospital.

On the floor, next to the Waller's hand, was a blue Smith & Wesson .357 Magnum Model 19 with wood handgrips. The weapon was then standard issue for our department and most other law enforcement in our area. There were three spent rounds and three remaining rounds in the chamber.

While checking out those two bodies, our officers had found another body, a middle-aged woman, under the covers on the bed. An upended walker lay on the floor by the bed.

Her chest was bloodied. She had been stabbed repeatedly, not with a knife, but, as we later discovered, with an awl—a tool about five inches long, used for punching leather. She was still there when I arrived. I touched her neck, and her body was cold.

We had three killed in the house, and another in the parking lot. At first inspection, Hank Waller appeared to have taken his own life after murdering the three others. But there was one nagging question.

The kitchen table was set for five. Who was missing?

Just then our crime scene guys reported that they'd found a note inside Linde Moore's car. It said, "I'm still having trouble with Bob."

The victim's husband was Robert Moore.

I turned to one of my detectives, pointed at the glasses on the table, and said, "Find that missing m-f."

NEXT OF KIN

Word had spread of multiple murders in the complex. Television satellite trucks, including CNN, were lining up outside. From photos in the house, I could see that there was at least one more daughter, Mary Elizabeth Waller, whom we had not yet located.

I called over another detective. "We need to find out where this woman and any other immediate family members are, so we can get to them before they see it on their local news."

Our guys identified and located the missing daughter. She was a registered nurse working in a hospital in New Mexico. I did not want her to be in a patient's room and look up at the television to see her parents' house labeled a murder scene.

I called the hospital and asked for the director of nursing.

"Hello, I am Detective Joe Kenda with the Colorado Springs Police Department. We are investigating a multiple-murder case involving the family of one of your nurses, Mary Elizabeth Waller."

I explained that she had lost her parents, her sister, and a nephew. I wanted to make sure she did not learn it from CNN while making her rounds.

"Oh, my God, I can't be the one to tell her," said the nursing director, her voice breaking.

I said, "Find her best friend on the nursing staff, tell her what happened, and then have her bring Mary to the phone for an urgent call. I want to tell her privately before she hears it somewhere else."

"Okay, I will do that."

I waited a good ten minutes on the phone while my gut did somersaults and jumping jacks.

"Hello?"

"Hello, Mary, this is Detective Sergeant Joe Kenda of the Colorado Springs Police Department."

"Yes," her voice was cracking already.

"I regret to inform you of a multiple homicide involving several of your family members. We are investigating a case in which your mother, sister, nephew, and father have all been killed. We are early into it, and we have no solid suspects at this point. I'm sorry, there is just no pleasant way to break that news to you. I assure you, however, that we are determined to find whoever did this, and bring them to justice."

She was a nurse, so she was emotionally tough, but nothing prepares you for a call like that. She broke down. Then she had several questions, which I answered as best I could at that point. I would never be able to answer all the questions that would haunt her dreams for the rest of her life.

As I completed that call, promising to keep her informed, one of my detectives notified me that he'd called Memorial Hospital looking for Linde Moore's husband, Robert, who worked there as a radiology technician.

"They said he wasn't working today," he said.

We already knew from a neighbor that the couple had recently separated.

"He might be the guy mentioned in the note found in the victim's car," I said. "And maybe he's the missing person at the breakfast table. Find him!"

Just then a patrol officer brought an older couple to me. He introduced them as the Sampsons, owners of the apartment complex.

"What can you tell me about the Wallers?" I said. "Any idea why this might have happened?"

"They were very nice people, happily married for thirty years or more, and we felt lucky to have them as resident managers," said Mr. Sampson.

Hank Waller was a retired junior high school social-studies teacher and former wrestling coach, a physically fit "gentle giant" who was beloved by students and fellow teachers. He was active at the Sunrise United Methodist Church and well liked by other residents of the apartment complex, where he also served as manager and handyman.

Later, I would learn that for twenty-six years, Hank had a second job in the summers as a special patrol officer on the Pike's Peak Highway. That explained the city-issued .357 Magnum. The city of Colorado Springs employed these special patrol officers to assist tourists traveling to and from one of the area's most popular attractions.

The nineteen-mile Pikes Peak Highway toll road climbed from an elevation of about seven thousand feet, just west of our city, to more than fourteen thousand feet, at the summit of Pikes Peak. The steep, winding drive took a couple of hours, and there were no gas stations on the route, so tourists were often running out of fuel or getting stuck because they wandered off the road.

We checked, and Hank Waller had still been working that part-time job, where he was highly regarded and often commended. His supervisor described him as "compassionate" and an excellent employee, whose only issue in the past few years was stressing out over little things too much.

Waller had been recognized for giving fifty dollars of his own cash to a needy couple whose vehicle broke down and stranded them. He had also been called a hero for stopping a car with failed breaks headed down from the mountain. He'd maneuvered his patrol vehicle in front of it and allowed the out-of-control car to ram the back of it as he braked, probably saving lives in the process.

A fellow patrol officer called him "the strongest man you could ever meet."

The Sampsons also held Waller in high regard, which made this case all the more baffling. In fact, they said their respect for Hank Waller had grown over the years, especially after Ola Mae was diagnosed with multiple sclerosis and confined to a wheelchair.

"Hank always called Ola Mae 'my bride,'" Mr. Sampson said. "He took really good care of her, serving as her primary caregiver. He had to lift her out of the chair to put her to bed or go to the bathroom. He never complained about it. He continued to care for her even after he had his stroke a couple years ago."

"A stroke?" I asked.

"Yes," Waller's employer said. "That's why he retired from teaching, which he missed a lot. For a while, his speech was slurred and he had trouble concentrating, but he recovered and continued to work, even though he still had some paralysis on his left side and couldn't use his left arm for much. We had noticed that recently he slowed down some. He talked slower, too, but he was still a good worker and always pleasant."

The Sampsons said they couldn't imagine why anyone, especially Hank Waller, would kill his wife and daughter and grandson.

But they did note that Waller, a very traditional Christian who did not believe in divorce, had become distressed over Linde's split with her husband. He and Ola were such doting parents that they had moved into the apartment complex after giving their own home to Linde and Bob.

"He was the type who would do anything to make a marriage work, and he couldn't understand why his kids wouldn't work harder to save theirs," Mrs. Sampson told a local newspaper.

NAGGING QUESTIONS

At that point, I thought it was entirely possible that Hank Waller had killed his daughter, his wife, his grandson, and himself. We had the neighbor's report of seeing him arguing with his daughter just before the shot was fired. We'd found him in the room with his gun and his murdered wife and grandson.

At that point, we had two big questions: (1) Why would this seemingly normal and well-liked guy kill his loved ones and himself? (2) And where was Bob Moore, the estranged husband of Linde and father of Brandon, and what role, if any, did he have in their murders?

I had detectives digging into Waller's background, looking for any clues to what might have driven him to commit these murders. So, I headed to Memorial Hospital with two of my guys to see what else we could find out about the one missing family member, Bob Moore.

We went to the hospital administrator's office and said we were looking for information on him since we couldn't find him.

"But Bob is here, working," the administrator said.

"We called, and they said he wasn't in," I said.

"Yes, apparently the person who answered your call had the impression that he wasn't scheduled today, but he came in around eight a.m.," the administrator said.

"Well, we'd like to talk to him right away," I said.

Word had not yet reached Moore about the killings, so we had the unenviable task of breaking the news to him that he'd lost his wife, son, and in-laws.

"There's no easy way to tell you this," I said. "Your wife and son were murdered early this morning. Linde's parents are also dead, and we are conducting a homicide investigation."

You never know how people will respond in these cases. I always prepare myself for the worst, which can include them attacking me or going into a rage. I've also seen people turn ice cold and show no emotion at all.

Bob Moore had a classic grief-stricken response. He broke down, first in disbelief and then in deep sobs. He was an emotional wreck.

I've learned that this response doesn't necessarily mean that the person was not involved in a murder. You never know until all the facts are gathered. But he certainly seemed both shocked and torn apart. He kept breaking down throughout our talk.

He admitted that he and his wife had been separated for a week due to strains in their relationship, and they had discussed divorce. He said Linde's parents, especially her father, had been upset about their marital problems and was opposed to a divorce.

"They want us to get back together, and we've talked about that, too," he said. "Her father has tried to get us back together. In fact, he asked me to come over for breakfast this morning, and Linde called to see if I could make it. But I had to go in to work, and really, I didn't want to get into it with her father."

Well, that explained the fifth place setting at the breakfast table. Bob was invited but had decided not to come. Still, I wasn't ready to eliminate him yet.

"Would you submit to a gunshot-residue test?"

"Yeah, of course," he said.

I told him to forget it. He had an alibi. He'd clocked in at work around eight a.m., which was about the same time Linde was shot. A bunch of coworkers and supervisors backed that up. And he was being cooperative despite his obvious grief.

The estranged husband appeared to be off our very short list of suspects. That left us with Hank Waller, but we still had no idea why the apparently decent and loving guy would have killed his wife, daughter, and grandchild and then himself.

A TORMENTED MIND

Bob Moore had said his father-in-law was tortured by the potential breakup of his daughter's marriage, but as it turned out, even Bob did not fully grasp the torment that Hank Waller had been going through.

In their interviews with family friends and neighbors, our guys were hearing that Waller's normally upbeat state of mind had darkened considerably in recent months. One of his close friends said that Waller even blamed himself for his daughter's marital problems.

Bob Moore and others noted that Waller had suffered a stroke two years earlier and had bouts of depression ever since. Some suspected that he had then suffered a series of ministrokes. The wiring in his brain was shorting out, and he became tortured.

He had sought therapy to help him handle dark thoughts. Moore said his father-in-law often became distraught, despondent, and even paranoid, due to sudden mood shifts.

"It's almost like he's become a manic-depressive," Moore said. "He has these big mood swings, and the slightest thing can set him off, even if you just look at him wrong."

Moore added that his father-in-law had treated him like a son and that they had always gotten along well until the recent separation.

"He called me the other night, and he was crying about our marriage issues. He said I should call him if I ever needed someone to talk to, but then he added something I found strange," Moore said.

"What was that?" I asked.

"He said, 'When one of us bleeds, we all bleed.'"

I have to admit, hearing that gave me the screaming willies, and I'm not a guy who gets creeped out easily. But this case soon grew even creepier.

Our crime scene team found the leather awl believed to be the murder weapon used on Ola Mae Waller. It was in a tray of keys in the Wallers' living room. More disturbing were the strange notes discovered around the Wallers' apartment. All appeared to have been written by Hank.

In one scrawled note that seemed to have been written just after, or even during, the killings, he apologized "for what has happened." He also provided the name of his attorney, who had written his will, and a phone number for his other daughter, living in New Mexico.

We couldn't say for certain if this qualified as a suicide note, but we soon found other notes that seemed to support the theory that Hank Waller had gone mad.

The "kill list" notes were especially chilling. I'd never seen anything quite like them. We found some tucked inside magazines around the house, and others in trash cans.

There were notes to kill the president, the governor, and the mayor, as well as more personal "kill" messages that named Bob, Ola Mae, Linde, Brandon, and Hank as the targets.

All these appeared to be in Hank Waller's handwriting, which certainly cast him in a darker state of mind than the "compassionate" husband, father, and grandfather we'd heard about.

Most observers, in law enforcement or otherwise, might have homed in on the son-in-law, Bob Moore, as the likely suspect in this case. And certainly, I've worked many homicide investigations where the estranged husband or boyfriend did turn out to be the killer.

But that is why I always preach to my detectives and others I train that you cannot jump to conclusions on any case. You have to follow the evidence to wherever it leads you, without making assumptions.

The evidence in this homicide investigation kept leading us to the far more unlikely but undeniable conclusion that Henry "Hank" Waller, a respected former teacher, a part-time lawman, and an admired family man, had murdered three family members and then taken his own life.

Now, throughout this investigation, we certainly kept in mind that perhaps someone had set Waller up, using very elaborate measures. However, we did have an eyewitness neighbor who looked out her window and saw the complex manager arguing with his daughter in the parking lot just seconds before the fatal shot was fired.

That would be hard to fake. Not impossible, but very difficult.

On top of that, we had the "kill lists," with handwriting that matched an unsent letter to Mary Elizabeth Waller, which talked about "a bad thing" that Bob Moore had done, and other family issues. It was signed, "Love, Dad."

We talked to Mary Elizabeth about that letter and her father's state of mind. She said that her mother had been telling her for months that there was something wrong with Hank. The sister in New Mexico also told us that her father had called her recently and seemed despondent over Linde's separation from her husband.

"He was saying really, really irrational things like 'I can't allow this to happen.' And 'They'll never stop me from seeing my grandson.'"

We also had multiple reports, from others who knew Waller well, that his mental state had become increasingly darker and more volatile since his stroke four years earlier. Waller had broken down while telling his pastor that he was depressed about his wife's advancing multiple sclerosis, their financial challenges, and his daughter's marital problems, especially if the breakup would mean less time with his grandson.

Another friend told us that Hank was so upset about Linde's breakup that he was planning to take her out of his will and leave only his wife, Mary Elizabeth, and Brandon as his beneficiaries.

We did talk to a psychiatrist about Hank Waller's stroke and the impact it might have had on his mental state. The shrink told us that strokes have been known to dramatically alter the personalities and behaviors of their victims.

I concluded that Mr. Waller felt he'd lost control of his family and his life and that he had decided to kill not only his wife, daughter, and grandchild, but also his son-in-law, Bob Moore. That is why he had invited him over for breakfast on the morning when all the killings occurred.

Who knows what might have happened if Moore hadn't gone to work? He might well have died, too, or he might have prevented at least some of the deaths.

We surmised that Linde had declined to sit down to breakfast, and her father had confronted her as she went to her car. They argued briefly, and he shot her. Then he returned to the house and did the rest of the killings.

Including his innocent grandson—a true act of depravity, and perhaps one that Waller could not live with on his conscience, so he put the gun to his own head and pulled the trigger.

Sheer madness.

LOSS PREVENTION

A week after we closed our investigation in this case, I received an invitation to speak to the Wallers' grieving family and friends at Sunrise United Methodist Church, where Henry's funeral was being held.

I was probably not the best choice to be anyone's grief counselor—I struggled with my own job-induced demons—but as a public servant, I accepted the invitation out of duty. Given the tragic aspects of this case in which a man chose to murder his wife, daughter, and grandson, speaking publicly was not an easy thing for me to do, as you probably can understand.

I was also aware of the fact that grieving family members can have conflicted feelings about the homicide detectives who worked a case. Some are grateful. Others blame us or see us as uncaring.

So when I walked into this gathering of about thirty silent, staring people, I feared they thought of me as the bad guy in the room. Within seconds, however, a young woman approached me in tears and gave me a crushing hug.

"I'm Mary Elizabeth Waller," she said. "I want to thank you so much for reaching out and telling me about this before I learned it from some other source. Ten minutes after you called, the news was on televisions all over the hospital."

"Yes, I was afraid of that," I told her. "I'm so sorry we couldn't tell you in person."

In speaking to her and the others, I did not try to make sense of these senseless acts.

"I just wish it were under better circumstances. What happened to the members of your congregation was a tragedy. The person you knew and loved is not the person who did this. A stroke unraveled the personality of Hank Waller, to the point of lunacy. I hope that in the future, other families will recognize the signs of mental illness and get professional help for the individual who is suffering.

"You don't want to go through this sort of tragic and senseless loss."

This was a fairly rare case back then—one in which an upstanding family man, a doting husband, father, and grandfather, turned into a murderous lunatic after suffering a series of strokes that altered his personality. But over the years, I handled many homicides in which the killer suffered from a mental illness of some sort.

The takeaway from this case, in my talk to those grieving friends and family, is that if someone you care about begins acting out of character—and especially if they seem to be depressed, paranoid, and withdrawn from their normal lives—please stage an intervention of some sort, for their safety and the safety of others. Tell them you want to take them to lunch or for ice cream, and then drive them to an appointment with a licensed therapist or counselor who can diagnose their problems and get them help.

The sad truth is that our country's mental health systems have all but collapsed due to negligence and neglect by our government. There are very few safety nets remaining out there, and those that remain are severely frayed.

The one large public mental-health facility in the Colorado Springs area was seeing four thousand people a month the last time I checked. And those are just the people who understand that there is something wrong with them and they need help. Many people who could benefit from professional care end up on the streets and homeless because they can't afford it, they can't access it, or they don't know how to find it.

Stephen King said, "Horror is the coming undone of something good," and that can happen more easily than you might think.

Our mental health system has come undone, and horrors have resulted. And in this tragic case, Hank Waller, known to his friends as "the gentle giant," was a good man who came undone and took his innocent loved ones with him.

MY SECRET STALKER

Just as an aside to this sad case, I once had a mentally deranged stalker who told a bunch of people that she wanted to kill "Kenda the cop." I'd never had any contact with her, as far as I knew.

She had probably seen my name and photograph in the newspapers or on television. This was in the early 1990s, when we had a big run of homicides and I was always doing interviews.

This woman, who lived in an east-side apartment in Colorado Springs, was fine when she took her meds, but whenever she went off them, she got loopy and determined to take me out.

She was a tiny little thing, and none of her neighbors took her seriously, so nobody bothered to warn me. Then she showed up at police headquarters one day, looking for yours truly and packing a semiautomatic Ruger Mini-14 assault rifle with a thirty-round magazine.

This was a serious weapon that could tear your ass in half. She had stolen it from a neighbor and came to the police department waving it around and screaming, "Kenda is a dead man!"

Some guys have groupies; I had a crazed would-be assassin.

Fortunately for my killer wannabe—and for me and other CSPD members—she had no idea how to chamber a round in that weapon, and our heroic officers on the front line at headquarters promptly disarmed her. They were well within their rights to shoot her on the spot, but she hadn't yet aimed the rifle at anyone, which saved her skin. When they had her in cuffs, they asked her why she wanted to kill me.

"Everybody hates that cop Kenda," she said.

I'm told one of my fellow officers replied, "Well, we hate him, too, but we haven't tried to shoot him—yet."

CHAPTER FOUR:
THE CHOIRBOY GONE BAD

THE TRIGGER: RAGE, REVENGE, AND MONEY

I have a friend who was a master of disaster. He spent years working in areas devastated by hurricanes, tornadoes, floods, and fires. He had to quit when the images began to haunt him.

He couldn't walk or drive anywhere without picturing destruction. He'd go through a perfectly normal, nice neighborhood, and his mind would send images of it ripped apart. Bodies in trees and shrubs. Houses shredded or burned to the ground. Trees toppled. Power lines down. Gas and water lines ruptured.

I understood perfectly. It was the same for me and most veteran homicide detectives. Everywhere we go, we expect to encounter murder and mayhem, even in "normal" suburban neighborhoods with white picket fences and neatly trimmed yards.

As I used to tell new recruits at the police academy, violence can happen anywhere, and it can come from anyone. There is no one profile for a murderer. They come in all shapes and sizes, all colors, all religions, all ages, and all socioeconomic levels. We learn to prepare ourselves for the worst from every person, in every environment and in any situation.

It's not that we are demented, pessimistic, or cursed souls. We simply live with the knowledge that cruelty and violence can happen anywhere, at any time, even in the most seemingly serene settings.

And so it was in this case.

The Limbricks were known as a hardworking, churchgoing family living the American dream. They had a nice two-story red-brick house, guarded by a giant maple tree, on Potter Street in a middle-class Colorado Springs neighborhood.

Charles was a long-distance trucker, which kept him on the road for weeks at a time. His wife, Betty Jean, drove a school bus and held other jobs while raising their three daughters to adulthood.

Their youngest child and only son, Chuck Jr., was still at home, attending junior high school. He was a good student and known as the best singer and musician in his school and his church. He'd been something of a musical prodigy. He began playing drums in his church band at the age of five. Three years later, he added the bass guitar to his repertoire.

Chuckie and his mother shared a musical bond. She loved to sing gospel music in the church choir. He loved to sing with her and even wrote songs about her. Chuckie would later recall of his mother, "Music brought her a lot of relief from, you know, the pain she probably was feeling in her life."

After saying that, he declined to explain the origins or source of her pain. Some would claim later that there was marital turmoil in the outwardly peaceful Limbrick home. Some even raised questions about infidelity on both sides.

We considered that scenario as the possible trigger in this case, but in truth, we never quite figured out what set off the killer. This one was a cypher. A lot of people who saw the good in Chuckie were shocked when the bad appeared.

And his dark side showed up time after time until, finally, after he'd caused a lot of pain, suffering, and death, his time ran out.

MIDDLE-CLASS MURDER

When forty-two-year-old Betty Jean Limbrick was murdered in September 1988 in her own home, neighbors expressed shock and grief.

She seemed like an all-American mom with a lot to live for. But when we took the call and went to her home, the much-admired Betty Jean was facedown at the foot of the stairs in the lower hallway of their split-level home and very much dead.

Nearly all the blood in her body had drained out and pooled around her.

"She was so well respected," a neighbor told me. "She didn't have an enemy in the world."

"Well, no," I said. "She had one enemy: the person who shot her, not once but twice, and killed her."

Betty Jean typically came home after the morning shift driving a District 11 school bus, took a little break, and returned to drive her load of kids home after school. She didn't make the second shift this time.

Her son had found her, according to the patrol officers at the scene when I arrived.

"Where's he?" I asked.

The officer pointed to Chuck Limbrick, and my first impression was not a good one. He was sitting on the front-porch steps, with his head against a column, sound asleep.

Chaos reigns all around him. Flashing lights, cops, reporters, and ambulance crews. And the kid who just found his mother shot to death in their home is sleeping peacefully on the porch?

That's not cool. It's cold.

"Wake his ass up, and put him in a squad car. I don't want anybody talking to him until we are ready," I said.

Then I noticed that one of our detectives had another kid in a squad car, talking intensely with him.

"Who's that?" I asked the patrol officer.

"That's the son's buddy. He was with him when they found her."

The kid looks like a dog shitting razor blades. He's shaking and bawling and jabbering away. The detective with him looked out the window of the squad car, made eye contact with me, and gave a thumbs-up.

I liked that. The buddy was shaken up, and he was a talker.

CRIME SCENE

I found it helpful to inspect a crime scene before talking to any witnesses, victims, or suspects. I like to form my own impression of what went down before hearing their stories.

I walked in the house—neatly kept, not flashy, but nice enough. I walked down a short flight of stairs to the lower level, where Mrs. Limbrick's body remained. The walls around her had blood spray on them, which is indicative of a high-velocity bullet wound. The gunshot produced a cloud of blood, a red mist, causing the spatter pattern.

The blood pool around the body was difficult to avoid as I bent down to make a preliminary check of her fatal wounds. I hated stepping in blood, for all sorts of reasons, but sometimes there was no other way to get to the victim.

I practically had to squat down in it to examine her head wound, a single-entry close-contact gunshot to the left temple. The gun had to be only inches from her head when fired. Now, that might have been an indication of a suicide, except that there was also a gunshot wound in her right hand and shoulder. The bullet entered at the joint of her middle finger and exited from her palm, then went through her shoulder.

The hand shot was likely the first. The second shot, fired directly into her head at close range, looked like something an assassin would administer.

This was not something you'd expect to see done to a hardworking, churchgoing mother of four in middle America. The weapon was a serious piece of firepower: a .357 Magnum.

READING THE SIGNS

This woman thought to lack enemies had suffered an extremely violent attack at the hands of someone who made sure she did not survive it. This looked like a personal vendetta killing to me, one in which the killer knew the victim and, for whatever reason, hated her.

Unlike so many of the homicides I'd handled, this one did not serve up an immediate list of likely suspects. The victim did not live in a high-crime area teeming with violent criminals and drug abusers. She did not stay out late at night in bars, nightclubs, or strip joints.

Had she come home and encountered an intruder, or a burglary in progress? That was one potential scenario. Another possibility, as mentioned earlier, was that Mrs. Limbrick did have an enemy, and not just someone who coveted her church pew or wanted her bus-driving job.

This enemy wanted her dead and gone from this world. Who could hate sweet-natured Betty Jean Limbrick that much?

Our investigation was already hindered by the fact that the killer had at least a two-hour head start on our investigation. You may have heard me mention this before, but I hate giving bad people a head start.

Call me competitive if you must, but I do not like being late to the starting line. That gives the killer too much time to toss the weapon into a river, drive a hundred miles from the murder scene, or dream up a decent alibi.

I would have been perfectly okay with setting up a hotline for local killers. They could have called me immediately after dispatching their victims, thus eliminating any lag time in my pursuit of them. Maybe that was hoping for too much, but a guy can dream, can't he?

I'd finished my preliminary examination of the victim's wounds when one of our officers asked me to come upstairs. Our search had turned up Mrs. Limbrick's purse, which appeared to have been rifled. The zippered pockets of her wallet were all open, and while several credit cards were present, along with her driver's license, there was no cash in her wallet.

For all I knew at that point, Mrs. Limbrick was a proud member of our cashless society, but the condition of her purse and contents suggested someone had gone through it in a hurry.

We came upon additional evidence supporting the possibility that the victim may have interrupted a burglary in progress. A couple of lamps were turned over and some furniture moved around. Even so, we didn't find clothes thrown out of closets, or drawers dumped upside down, which is usually the case in residential burglaries.

At first, we couldn't find any sign of forced entry, but our crime scene team did find a screen pulled off an open rear window to the house. There were footprints in the dirt under it. They photographed them and made molds for evidence.

While I was taking note of all this, my guys reported that Mrs. Limbrick's car was nowhere to be found. We'd been told she usually parked it in the garage, but it was not there.

I had my guys put out a bulletin on the missing car and its license plate number, notifying all law enforcement agencies in the state and region that we were looking for the vehicle.

We were also looking for the husband, Charles Limbrick senior, whom we hadn't been able to reach. A neighbor gave us the name of the trucking company he drove for, and we had them track him down for us. He was eight hundred miles away, which is the start of a good alibi, but we needed to check it out, certainly.

We'd picked up some rumors that the Limbricks were having marital difficulties, and there were even reports of an affair—or two. Nobody had any names or eyewitness accounts of strangers showing up late at night when Charles was on the road. So we took notes and filed them in our brains for future reference.

Charles senior was on our list of potential suspects, especially after a neighbor told us he'd been talking about buying a handgun, ostensibly for his wife's protection while he was on the road.

Being interested in buying a gun for your wife doesn't make you a killer, but it kept him high on the list of people we wanted to talk to. The annals of crime over the centuries certainly contain cases in which a jealous or wandering husband shoots his wife and then tries to make it look like a burglary gone bad.

If a guy was looking to kill his wife and put a lot of miles between the murder scene and himself, a veteran long-haul trucker would know how to put the pedal to the metal and skedaddle.

A COOL CUSTOMER

Once we'd checked on the whereabouts of the victim's husband and completed the preliminary search of the home and the victim, I turned to interviewing the teenage son, who had called us after discovering her body in their home.

Charles Limbrick Jr., known as "Chuck" or "Chuckie" to family and friends, was widely hailed as a promising young musician and singer. He was charismatic and popular, according to neighbors and classmates we had interviewed along their street.

I told my guys to keep that in mind when we talked to him the first time. After finding him asleep on the porch after his mother's murder, I wasn't impressed. But maybe I had him wrong.

People respond to tragedy in different ways. Teenagers are strange even in normal situations. All those raging hormones and unwired brain paths can result in odd behavior. So I cut him some slack, figuring he'd been through a horrific situation—one of the worst I could imagine.

"Chuck, I know this is a horrible time for you, and I'm sorry for this interruption, but I'm leading this investigation," I said. "We want to find the person who did this and bring him to justice. So I need you to tell me how you found your mother."

He'd been crying and tried to gather himself, but he sputtered only a few words out before he choked up. He took a minute, then offered a quick summary of the day's events.

Chuck and his friend Chris had met after school and gone to the Citadel Mall. They left there and went to Chuck's home, but it was locked up. They went to the home of a neighbor, Bill Robinson, who kept an extra key to their house for just such occasions.

The buddy, Chris, had stayed outside with Robinson when Chuck went back and opened the front door to the house. Chuck said he found his mother dead and called for his neighbor and his friend to come in the house.

The kid lost it at that point. We didn't push him. There would be time to dig into his story later. I thought it sounded a little too pat.

My initial opinion of him was confirmed by his response when I expressed sympathy over his mother's death.

"Yeah," he said.

Yeah? Oh, my, you are a cold fish, choirboy.

That didn't seem like a really heartfelt response.

There is an expression in law enforcement represented by the initialism JDLR. "Just Doesn't Look Right." This was one of those JDLR situations.

HITTING THE TARGET

With the on-the-road husband ruled out, our investigation was going nowhere fast, but then some more welcome automotive news arose.

One of our patrol units called in, reporting they had found the victim's car just two miles from the Limbrick home.

Thanks, I needed that.

I headed to its location, outside a Target store in a shopping center parking lot. Our crime scene team went over it, looking for fingerprints, traces of blood, a weapon—anything that might help us identify the suspect, who, we assumed, stole it and drove it to this spot.

They turned up nothing to help the case, but just the location of the car interested me. Why would the killer drive it only a couple of miles before ditching it? Why take it at all if that was as far as you wanted to go?

Now, maybe the killer had another car, the proverbial getaway car, parked at the Target store. Or maybe our suspect stole another car there and took off. But stealing the car after murdering its owner seemed a risky move. If someone had seen the driver in the car, it would link that person directly to the murder. Why take that risk?

I couldn't come up with many good reasons for heading to Target after committing a murder. Then again, I can't think of many good reasons for going shopping. I'm not a shopper. I do my hunting and gathering on the job.

The car's location was an odd twist in the case. We followed it up by canvassing employees and assorted mall rats in hopes of finding someone who had seen the driver park it.

Back then security cameras weren't everywhere as they are today. If this had happened in more recent times, we probably could have found some footage of the car and driver traveling between the murder scene and the Target parking lot.

The widespread use of security cameras has been a boon to law enforcement in that regard. I know that people complain about privacy violations, but my response is, "If you don't break any laws, why would you worry?"

Checking security cameras would be one hell of a lot easier than trying to find someone who had seen a single car pull into a three-thousand-space parking lot a day or two earlier. It would have been helpful if Mrs. Limbrick had owned a cherry-red Maserati or even a zebra-striped Ford Explorer—something that stood out from all the other vehicles.

But she didn't. She drove a typical working-mom car, a 1976 Buick Limited. Four-door, white top, blue body. A General Motors generic car. They probably sold a couple hundred thousand of them. And millions of others that looked just like them.

We turned up a few regulars who had noticed her hardly noticeable car because they parked nearby, but they all had different timelines of when it showed up.

This is why many detectives go bald from tearing out their hair. Fortunately for my own locks, I was more of a nail biter. Real nails. Steel. I chew 'em and spit out bullets.

My dentist loved it, by the way. The cost of my broken molars put his kids through college.

LET'S HEAR IT FOR NOSY NEIGHBORS

We had hit another dry pothole, so to speak, with Betty Jean's car. When an investigation is headed nowhere, I like to go back to the scene of the crime and take a fresh look. We knocked on more doors, hoping to find someone who might not have been home on our first neighborhood canvass. It's low-tech, shoe-leather-and-sore-knuckles police work, but sometimes there's a big payoff.

This was one of those times.

"Hey, Sergeant Kenda, you're gonna like this. I'm at the house across the street from the Limbricks', and a juvenile female here says she's got some info on the case."

I love it when that happens.

Let's call her Nikki DeVecchio. My new favorite gum-chewing teeny-bopper of the moment said that when she was coming home from school on the day of the murder, she'd seen Betty Jean's car driving by. She knew Chuck and his mom, and she knew the car.

"I was expecting to see Mrs. Limbrick in the car, but instead I saw Chuck driving," she told me. "I couldn't see who the passenger was, but I definitely saw Chuckie."

Well, well, well, isn't that interesting!

Neither Chuck nor his friend Chris had mentioned going for a drive in her car before—or after—finding the victim. And Chuck wasn't old enough to drive.

With a little polite prompting, Nikki added that Chuck and his mother argued a lot, and Chuck had talked about running away, many times. She said she'd often smelled beer on his breath, and while he was drinking, she had heard him talk about hating his mom.

"One time, I playfully punched him on the arm, and he got mad. He told me to never hit him again," Nikki said. "Then he told me, 'My mom hit me once, and she'll never do that again, either.'"

The helpful neighbor added that Chuck's pal, Chris Marrow, was in her eighth-grade history class and had a bad reputation.

"He gets in trouble a lot, and I think he's been arrested," she said.

We hadn't gotten around to checking young Marrow's name in juvenile records, but after our talk with Nikki D., it seemed like a good idea.

As it turned out, Nikki was right.

THE WINGMAN

Our initial interview with Chuck Limbrick's sidekick hadn't given us any answers and, in fact, raised more than a few questions. Chris Marrow had given us the same pat description of events on the day of the murder.

All you true-crime fans out there know what I was thinking. It's very rare for two witnesses to offer exactly the same account of an event, even if they were together. Unless they've gone over their stories and practiced them for some reason—and it usually isn't a good reason.

We had also learned that Marrow wasn't just a bad boy poseur pretending to be Fonzie Fonzarelli. Just recently, he'd been caught up in an auto-theft investigation. Our guys had arrested him, and under questioning, he'd given up the names of some key players. It wasn't exactly grand theft auto—more like joyriding—so he walked away without any charges after cooperating.

We liked that Limbrick's buddy had been helpful to a past police investigation. That gave us hope in a dark and cold world. We always looked forward to talking to a known thief who didn't mind throwing a friend or coworker under the bus. This was our kind of guy.

Mr. Marrow had some explaining to do. He wasn't a suspect in the murder (yet), but I suspected that he had lied to me in our first conversation at the Limbrick home—or at least omitted the fact that he'd been joyriding in Betty Jean's car. But maybe he didn't think that was important. I intended to set him straight on that point and probably many others.

It's always helpful to talk with friends and family before directly confronting a key witness or suspect. You want to know as much about them as possible. So I paid his parents a visit.

I chatted up Mr. Marrow for several minutes, discussing his son's previous run-ins with our department, his school activities, and his overall attitude.

Then I popped a more critical question: "Mr. Marrow, do you own a handgun?"

"Oh, yeah, I do," he said.

"Would you mind bringing it to me now?" I asked, though it was really more of a demand, which is one of the things we in law enforcement are allowed to do.

The father left the room, went up the stairs, and, I presume, rummaged through his sock drawer looking for his pistol. Then he returned empty-handed, with a worried look on his face.

"I can't find it," he said. "It's not where I always keep it."

He seemed genuinely frazzled.

I asked to see his paperwork on the gun. He produced the documentation and made my day. It was a Smith & Wesson Model 19 .357 Magnum revolver with a six-inch barrel.

As you may recall, dear reader, the slugs found at the Limbrick home were also from a .357 Magnum pistol. We also asked Mr. Marrow if he had a box of ammunition for the gun and if that was missing, too.

Yes, and yes, he said.

Our crime scene guys had found a box of cartridges for a .357 Magnum pistol in Chuckie's bedroom.

With those revelations, my detective brain began whirling with all that I'd learned about the teenage Marrow. He was a close friend of Chuckie Limbrick and a frequent visitor to the family home.

He'd been at the murder scene when the body was recovered. He had previous encounters with our department, and access to a pistol that matched the murder weapon.

"Mr. Marrow, I'd like to talk to your son again," I said. "Now."

You can imagine how the father took that request.

"Why? Do you suspect he was involved in the murder of Mrs. Limbrick? With *my gun*? That couldn't be true! Maybe we should call a lawyer now?"

They seemed like nice people, so I didn't shoot them.

Just kidding.

I mean, about the shooting them part.

"I'm not saying Chris is a suspect at this time," I said. "I simply have a few questions for him, and you can sit here while I ask them."

Mr. Marrow had his son come down from his room.

The teen did not look thrilled to see me.

"Chris, I have a few more questions for you regarding Mrs. Limbrick's killing. I want you to think hard and give me your best, honest recollections of that day. Okay?"

A sullen teenage nod was all I got in reply.

"So take me through the day, step-by-step after you arrived at Chuck's house."

He spewed the same story pretty much on the mark. The kid came to class prepared, I gave him that. He was a well-schooled liar. And I am a well-schooled lie detector.

While he was reciting his web of lies, I gave him a reappraisal, figuring out how to crack this nut. Then I noticed his shoes, and it clicked. We found footprints under the window used to enter the Limbrick home.

"Those are pretty nice shoes you got there, Chris. Let me see them, please."

He sullenly extended his leg and gave me a profile of his kicks.

"No, take off that shoe."

"I don't want to take off my shoe," he said.

Wrong answer.

"Either you take it off, son, or I'll take it off."

Chris saw the light. He took off the sneaker and handed it to me.

I turned it over and examined the tread. Actually, I only pretended to examine it, because I had no idea what our footprint from the crime scene looked like. I hadn't committed it to memory. But I wanted the kid to *think* I was Sherlock Holmesing his ass.

I didn't say anything. I studied the shoe. He studied me.

"Wouldn't you find it strange if your shoe's tread matches the one we found under a window at the Limbrick house—the same window the killer used to enter the house?"

"A lot of people have these same shoes," he said.

Obviously, the kid had already given this some thought.

"True, a lot of people have this shoe, but then, so do you, Chris. And you were there on the day Mrs. Limbrick was murdered."

That rattled his cage. His hands trembled. His legs danced.

Chris had cracked in the car theft case, and he was about to crack again because he knew he was in over his head on a murder case.

CHILD'S PLAY

There are approaches for interrogating juveniles and certain adult suspects who are not hardened criminals with nothing to lose. With them, you don't go for the jugular right off. You don't make "punishment" comments like, "Unless you tell me the truth, you are going to prison for the rest of your fucking life, and most of your afterlife, too!"

That doesn't work so well with the younger, softer suspects, because it either makes them start sobbing or makes their parents end the conversation with a call to their lawyer.

I taught my guys to use a more indirect approach in these cases. You come across more like the family's pastor than like a hard-ass cop. You build rapport with the kid and the parents so there is a certain level of comfort. You position yourself as someone who wants to help them get to the truth and relieve them of any guilt they might be carrying.

You keep them a little off balance so they lose focus, drop their guard, and make mistakes. Then you pounce on their ass. Chris was in his own home with his parents present. He liked to think he was a tough guy, but tough guys don't still live with Mom and Dad.

Nearly everyone involved in a murder wants to be understood and forgiven, even if they don't regret it. The difference between a detective like me and a priest is that I don't forgive and I don't forget. But I would use that need for understanding and forgiveness to extract the truth, and I encouraged the detectives who worked for me to do the same.

We actually take classes in this stuff, by the way. We don't just make it up as we go. Still, it is a complicated procedure and it doesn't always work. But when it does, you feel a real sense of accomplishment.

Confessions are relatively rare, especially if you're dealing with hard-nosed criminals, alcoholics, drug abusers, and sociopaths. Even so, veteran interrogators will tell you that if you spend enough time with your subject, you can figure out which buttons to push.

A veteran CIA interrogator once said, "I don't believe in torture, because it doesn't work, and I don't need it. Given enough time, I can get in someone's head and get everything I need from them."

My next question to the teenager was one taught in interrogation classes for law enforcement. The approach differs for each individual, or at least each type of individual. Chris had been in some trouble, but he was from a good family and he still had a conscience. He was mostly scared to tell the truth. After what he'd seen, he had good reason to be scared.

Teens and younger kids who haven't been hardened by abuse or deep poverty or racism are more likely to tell you the truth if you go at them after building a certain comfort level by asking about their daily life and activities.

Another method is to make statements that you know are false, or that you at least don't know are true. If you've prepared them properly, kids will sometimes blurt out the truth to correct you or set you straight, even if it incriminates them.

In this case, I kept asking Chris indirect, nonthreatening questions that gave him wiggle room, or so he thought. In truth, I was leading him through a maze that ended in a prison cell.

"What do you think ought to happen to the person who murdered Mrs. Limbrick?"

"He should go to prison and be punished forever."

"What should happen to somebody who maybe just knows about it but didn't do it?"

Chris fell silent at that one.

I was in the right church and getting close to the right pew. He didn't want to talk about that person, because he *was* that person.

It was time to bring down the soft hammer.

"You were there, weren't you?"

Now the kid was getting scared. He had never been in such a serious, life-changing moment. He may have taken a car for a joyride and done some other petty crimes, but this was murder. He'd been involved in a horrible and traumatic crime.

I could see the "tells," body movements that betray anxiety and fear. Professional poker players are skilled at reading them in the other players. I'm better at reading them in interrogation subjects.

Christopher's eyes were dancing, his facial muscles were twitching, and he couldn't keep his knees and feet still. He was hanging over the edge of the cliff. I offered him a rope. He thought it was for his safety. Silly kid.

"Okay, son. Here's what you are going to do. You are going to tell me the truth from here on out. Tell me what happened that day in the Limbrick home? And don't lie to me this time."

A true criminal would have told me to do something unnatural to myself and clammed up. Chris was not one of those guys—yet. He was all bluster and bullshit, but at heart, he was a scared kid. With his parents watching, it was even harder for him to lie to me.

The story poured out. It wasn't quite what I'd mapped out in my head, but close. His buddy Chuck had told him a month earlier that he wanted to run away because his parents, especially his mom, were too controlling.

Chuckie had decided he wanted to escape parental control and move to Canada. Christopher volunteered to go with him because he'd been in trouble for his involvement in the car theft ring. Chuck said Jasmine, a girlfriend, wanted to go with them, too.

What sort of plan was this? Get away to Canada? Maybe they thought they could tap trees and live off maple syrup. Or take up curling and get endorsements from . . . hell, I don't know. Who the hell watches curling, let alone endorses it?

These three idiots didn't really have a plan. They were spoiled adolescents whose brains were a thousand synapses short of rewiring. They didn't have passports or a clue.

Their lamebrain plan was to drive across the northern border in Limbrick's father's car, which was parked in the driveway since his dad was on the road in his truck.

It got worse. Dangerously worse.

On the morning of their planned getaway, Chuck called and asked his pliable buddy to bring "some protection."

"What do you mean?"

"Bring your father's gun."

Being a follower and a dolt, Chris swiped his father's gun from the closet and put it in his backpack before heading to Chuck's. They took the father's car, picked up Jasmine, and headed out, but they'd driven only a few blocks when Chuck saw his mom headed their way in her Buick.

Betty Jean was coming home between shifts on the school bus.

"We need to beat her home," said Chuckie.

Chris could not figure out why Chuck wanted to return to the house with his mother there, but he went along with the plan because he's a moron. They sped back and got there before Betty Jean pulled up in her car.

Chuckie told Jasmine to walk down the street and hang out until he came for her. He and Chris went around back so his mother wouldn't see them, and climbed in a window.

Then they waited for her downstairs. Before his mother walked in, Chuckie said to Chris, "Did you bring the gun?"

"Yeah, why?"

"Give it to me! I have to kill her or she'll come after us and bring us home!"

Chris said he didn't believe that Chuck would really shoot his own mother. But the stunned idiot handed his father's gun over to his friend and then hid in a bedroom.

Mrs. Limbrick walked in and said, "Chuckie, are you home?"

Chuckie did not answer. He stayed hidden downstairs.

Betty Jean came down the steps.

Chris heard the horrifying click of Chuckie pulling back the hammer of the pistol. Then he heard the explosive gunshot.

Betty Jean screamed and said, "Chuckie, I love you, but you just shot me!"

Then Chris heard a second shot, and the sound of Mrs. Limbrick falling to the floor.

As soon as he told me this, Chris Marrow's parents looked at him in horror.

"I came out of the bedroom and saw Mrs. Limbrick dead on the floor," he said. "Then Chuck told me to get some trash bags so we could dump her somewhere. But I said we needed to get out of there in case someone heard the shots."

At that point, Chuck decided to make it look like a burglary gone wrong. He did a half-assed job of that, toppling over a few pieces of furniture and taking the cash from his mother's purse, as well as her car keys.

They picked up Jasmine down the street but, after a brief discussion, took her home because Chuckie had decided not to go to Canada, for some reason. Chris couldn't explain either that or why Chuck decided to drive his mother's car to the mall and park it outside a Target store.

Apparently, Chuckie thought that was what a killer burglar would do. Maybe he liked the symbolism. Park the car at Target. Bull's-eye!

As Chris laid out the sprawling insanity of this murder, a rare matricide, I asked him why Chuckie would have killed his mother.

"She had grounded him a couple times because he refused to help out at home, and he hated her for it," Chris said. "About four months ago, Chuck took a wine cooler out of the refrigerator, and his mother caught him drinking it. She told him to stop. He called her a name. She slapped him in the face. He hated her for that. He told me he wanted to kill her."

Not to gloat, which is beneath my dignity, but my first impression of Chuckie the choirboy had been correct. He was a cold-blooded SOB. He'd probably skated through life on his charms and musical gifts and had grown to resent any of his mother's attempts to control him or get him to do work around the house.

Everything was fine with him, as long as you didn't say no.

There was one other question lingering at that point.

"Chris, what did Chuck do with the gun?"

"We took it to our school and hid it in a dumpster," he said.

Our guys found the gun registered to Chris Marrow's father there, at Emerson Junior High School, still in the brown holster. There were two expended casings.

Chuckie's fingerprints were all over it—a big oversight by the criminal mastermind.

We had all we needed.

Chuck's father was still on his way back from Louisiana when we took the son into custody. We found him at an aunt's house. We told him he was under arrest, then cuffed and searched him.

We found 114 dollars in cash in his shoe—the money he'd taken from his mom's purse after shooting her twice.

Now we had more than we needed.

When you put someone in jail, at the booking desk they are asked to fill out a simple information card listing the names and addresses of family members. This serves as an informal test to make sure the person isn't jacked up on some drug or otherwise screwed up. It can also tell us a bit about the person's state of mind.

Chuckie's cold heart came through. He listed his father's name and then, under his mother's name, he wrote, "Deceased."

This confirmed my suspicion that he was an adolescent sociopath. The kid was all charm, no heart. And no conscience.

His father seemed to feel the same way.

When Charles senior finally made it back to Colorado Springs, we already had his son locked up. The dad asked to see him, but from the tone of his voice, we decided that might not be a good idea.

"Just give me five minutes alone with that little fuck," he said.

Or words to that effect.

Chuckie was charged with first-degree murder and sentenced to life in prison. Chris Marrow was charged with second-degree murder and armed robbery. He pleaded guilty and was sentenced to eight years.

BLOWN CHANCES

In Colorado, we had a children's criminal code, a separate body of law. Anyone under eighteen is legally a child even though he might be a hulking middle linebacker on the high school football team. The rules said you had to be over twelve and have schemed, designed, shown malice, used a weapon, and caused death before you could be tried as an adult.

Chuckie qualified, so he was charged as an adult. He was a nice-looking kid, friendly, musically talented. You looked at him and he just seemed like a good guy you'd trust to date your daughter or dog-sit your beloved pooch.

He was a master at hiding his dark heart.

Even the notoriously hard-nosed prosecutor who put him in prison later told reporters, "I felt like Chuck had potential. This was a sad case, as heinous as the crime is."

At the age of fifteen, Chuckie became the youngest person ever locked up in the Colorado State Corrections System. That fact elicited no little wailing and gnashing of teeth from kindhearted but naive people who hadn't been shot twice and murdered by the killer choirboy.

They thought the police and the prosecuting attorney were evil for putting this youngster behind bars with predatory adult criminals. Believe me, Chuckie was nobody's prey. The kid had very strong survival instincts.

Normally, I don't care what happens to a killer once we get him convicted and locked up, but Chuckie's name kept popping up over the years. He used his musical talents to charm his fellow inmates and corrections officials, working with troubled kids in a prison program, teaching piano and guitar, and performing in prison shows.

One report said that Limbrick's Praise Team prison choir had become so popular that the number of inmates attending Sunday services doubled.

In fawning interviews, he made statements intended to impress the parole board. "I loved my mother and I think of her all the time," he said in a 2009 newspaper article with the headline "INMATE MAESTRO EARNS RESPECT IN PRISON."

"I don't even know how to relate to the person that I was, what, twenty-one years ago. Wow," he said in that puff piece.

Chuck Limbrick worked the system. It took him twenty-three years, but he finally charmed his way to freedom. Colorado Governor Bill Ritter commuted his sentence in 2011, just before leaving public office.

The public was grateful, until it wasn't.

Upon his release, Limbrick launched a Kickstarter fund-raising campaign to raise ten thousand dollars to pay for the recording of his gospel album entitled *I Made It,* by Chuck Limbrick "Mystro."

I found his plea for funding more than a little disturbing. Chuckie wrote that he'd always had a passion for music, but then, "My life changed forever when I was fifteen, and I made a mistake that would give me a life sentence in prison, and I became Colorado's youngest person at an adult correctional facility."

A mistake? You shot your mother twice with a .357 Magnum, and it was a simple mistake?

I could tell where this was headed, and true to form, Chuckie turned on the charm.

"After a couple years of being locked up, I decided that I wanted the Lord to use my life, my story, and my passion to bring glory to him. God was able to use all three during my twenty-three years in prison. I was able to lead worship music for the prison ministry, sing in the prison choir, and record two Christian CDs. I was able to use my story to serve as a warning to young people, as well as a testimony to God's incredible grace and redemption.

"I now have the freedom to use the gifts and story that God has given me to bring Him glory, so I am doing what I know how to do best: going to the studio . . . God is up to something big, and I would love for you to partner with me in this. Thanks for all your support and prayers. God bless you."

He raised more than ten thousand dollars, recorded the album, and sold it on iTunes and other places. He formed a band that played in local churches, and he gave more interviews.

I found it interesting that in those interviews, Chuckie always dodged the question about why he murdered his mother. Reporters tried to get it out of him, but he was a slippery devil.

"You ask a kid, 'Why did you take the cookie out of the cookie jar when I told you not to?' and the first thing he says is 'I don't know,' and the truth is, he really don't know," Chuckie said in one interview. "So you know, in scenarios that I've faced in my life sometimes, you know, the reality is, I don't know.

"I think that when you're a young person, you don't do things purposefully. You just, you act on impulse. You just do what you do.

"And that's what's happening to a majority of the kids out here today."

In another interview after his release, the choirboy said he'd been saved by the Lord and forgiven by his mother in heaven.

"I know my mama loves me, and I believe in my heart that she's proud of me for the person that I've become . . . I love her and I miss her, and I would tell her that I'm working to make her proud and make my family proud. I know I made some mistakes. I know there's probably a lot of people hurt by a lot of the choices and decisions that I've made, but I'm making it right, and I think that she already knows that."

Well, not quite, Chuckie boy.

He wasn't done making mistakes and bad decisions that hurt other people.

Just after eleven a.m. on March 4, 2015, while still on parole, he went for a drive after drinking coffee mixed with heavy doses of vodka. His

blood alcohol content was nearly three times the legal level of intoxication. That was a bad decision, and Jamie Northam paid the price.

Limbrick's car slammed into the back of her vehicle. Northam suffered
permanent facial scarring, traumatic brain and soft-tissue injuries, long-term
joint disorders, back damage, memory loss, and other health problems.

Despite all that, Northam and her husband told reporters that they
didn't want Chuckie to return to prison for the rest of his life. Jamie said
she felt sorry for him and had forgiven him.

That was her prerogative, of course. And the judge took it into account.
Chuckie did not go back to prison for the rest of his days. Instead, after
nearly killing another woman, he was ordered to complete a hundred
hours of community service, undergo alcohol education, and get a mental
health evaluation.

I'm sure Chuckie thought that his heavenly supporters were pleased
with that outcome. He probably felt that he'd been saved once again
despite all the pain, suffering, and death he'd caused.

But what happened next indicated to me that everyone in this world
and the next one, too, had had enough of Chuckie's bullshit.

About ninety days after his trial ended, Chuckie went for another
drive after drinking alcohol. This time, he didn't get to hurt anyone else.

The forty-four-year-old church musician and convicted murderer
rolled the vehicle and was thrown from the car because he wasn't wearing
a seat belt. State police said speed and alcohol contributed to the wreck
and to his death.

So long, Chuckie. You finally bit the big one. Couldn't have happened
to a more deserving guy. Some people die too soon. You didn't die soon
enough—in my book, at least.

CHAPTER FIVE:
A KILLER RENTAL

THE TRIGGER: GREED

After six years as the sergeant in charge of the homicide division, I'd been on call seven days a week for too long, according to Mrs. Kenda. She was more than a little annoyed with me. To avoid a messy divorce (Is there any other kind?) and return to some semblance of a normal family life, I asked for weekends off, and the chief agreed.

The problem was, I had to train my replacement, and it took forever to get the new guy to where he needed to be. His training took more than a year before I felt comfortable leaving him in charge of the Saturday-Sunday carnival of carnage.

Finally, at the end of the second week of January 1990, I turned him loose.

"Honey, I'm home!"

I'd really been looking forward to having a weekend when I could just relax, watch football, and have a couple of beers without death knocking on my door. That first Sunday was set up to be all the sweeter because the Denver Broncos were at home and taking on the Cleveland Browns in the NFL playoffs.

I actually get to watch a whole football game!

Or so I thought.

At eleven a.m., I settled into my favorite chair. The Browns kicked off to the Broncos. I was at peace with the world.

Then all hell broke loose.

As John Elway set up the offense for the first series of plays, the damned telephone rang.

This isn't going to be good news, I thought.

"Sarge, I'm at a house in the East Lakes neighborhood, and the chief is here and it looks like some sort of a religious ritual killing with bodies everywhere. Oh, my gawd, you gotta get over here!"

I hung up the phone and looked at my wife.

She gave me the one-finger salute, snatched away the beer I'd just opened, and took a big swig.

"I guess this is mine now," she said.

That was my cue to get out before she started throwing things at me. Kathy had a better arm than Elway, but the Broncos made it to the Super Bowl without her help.

My first Sunday off was over before the Broncos' first play from scrimmage. I really had to go to the crime scene. Our police chief never showed up unless the stakes were high.

I drove to the blue-collar neighborhood just east of downtown. It's never a good sign when every television satellite truck within a hundred miles is parked on the street before you arrive. It looked like the Super Bowl parking lot.

The chief was there, and all his chiefettes were running around like chickens with their heads cut off.

I asked the patrolman outside, "What the hell is this all about?"

"There's an altar in the house, an animal sacrifice, and an adult female and four kids dead."

Okay, that sounds bad.

I headed toward the front door to check it out for myself but ran into a small troop of top brass. They were all in a dither about the religious-sacrifice angle.

"I'm gonna go tell the press about this," said the chief.

"Okay, but let me take a look first before we say something to the press that we can't unsay later," I suggested.

Homicide investigations can go sideways fast if the press gets hold of a mere first impression of a crime scene, because often those first impressions are either flat-out wrong or not fully supported by the facts gathered later.

I knew that once newspaper headlines and television news reports started screaming "Religious sacrifice!" we'd have every nut job in the western United States flooding us with phone calls.

To prevent that from happening, I always tried to bring order to chaos. Step one: talk to the first officer at the scene.

I found him and pulled him aside.

"Okay, what have you got?"

"The neighbors say the woman believed to be the mother of the kids just rented the house and moved in five days ago," the patrolman said. "Her brother was trying to call her for a couple of days and couldn't get an answer. So this morning, he came to the house and found it all locked up. Windows and doors, with the blinds pulled down. But her car was parked outside and that worried him."

When the brother walked to the rear of the house, he found a back window where the blinds were not pulled all the way down. He could see a pair of legs sprawled on the floor.

"That's when he called 911, and I was dispatched to check it out," the officer said.

This is called a "welfare check," but it's not a government handout. We dispatch an officer to check on the welfare of a resident due to concerns expressed by neighbors or family members or the mailman. We do a lot of welfare checks. Most of them turn out to be nothing.

This one was really something.

"Everything was locked up tight," the patrolman told me. "But when I looked in the window, I saw someone down, too, so I used a knife to jimmy the window lock and climb inside."

He had to take a pause and gather himself before describing what he found. I'll warn you, it was disturbing.

There were five bodies: four children and an adult female. From the condition of their bodies, they had likely been dead three or four days.

One of the older kids was in the bathroom with his pants down. The others were still in bed. The mother was wearing a T-shirt and underwear, no pants.

"Then there was this sort of altar over the fake fireplace, with religious artifacts and pictures on it, and next to it was a dead cat," the patrolman said.

When he came out and reported what he'd seen to the patrol supervisor who had arrived, the supervisor hit the panic button and decided that what we had here was a ritualistic killing.

He put the call out, making it sound as if the Manson gang had struck again, which brought all the brass and media streaming in.

My impression was that the supervisor had been watching too many scary movies involving voodoo hoodoo.

"Okay, I have a few questions for you before I go in and take a look," I said to the patrol officer. "Did you check every door of the house?"

"Yes, totally secured."

"Any damage or indication of damage?"

"None."

"Is there a basement access?"

"No."

"So, you checked everything."

"Yes, sir."

"You say there is a dead cat on a plank?"

"Yes."

"Dead how? A knife in the chest? Gutted? How was it killed?"

"It just looks like it's asleep. No visible wounds."

"What about the people? Gunshot wounds, stab wounds, blood?"

"None of that . . . Well, there was a little blood coming from some of the victims' noses—like a bloody nose, not like a wound."

I went back to our band of brass wringing their hands over a ritual murder.

"You'd better not have a press conference yet."

"Why not?" asked one of the minions.

"Unless this is a homicidal Houdini, our killer could still be in the house, because it's all locked and sealed tight," I said. "The other alternative is that this was all done by an evil spirit that can pass through walls."

I was telling them that we needed to take a closer look before sounding the alarms and panicking the populace. My Spidey senses were telling me that this wasn't the kinky killing it had been cracked up to be.

"Oh, and the whole religious-ritual angle is looking like pure bullshit. But again, I'm going in to get a look at it all, so please, cool your jets."

The first officer on the scene had forced a window open, looked around the tiny place, and then quickly unlocked the front door and walked out. His training had taught him to get in and out quickly to lessen any chance of disturbing possible evidence.

My job was to look for that evidence while not screwing it up.

I went in through the front door and could pretty much see everything I needed to see. In the first room was the "altar," which was no more than a two-by-six board about eight feet long, suspended over bricks to create a mantel over the fake fireplace. The "religious artifacts" were the sort you'd find in many Hispanic homes. The Madonna portrait. Some prayer candles and other typical Christian decor.

The dead cat was just a dead cat. It hadn't been mutilated. There was no blood present. It looked asleep, but it was dead. No doubt about that.

It was a small house, so from the front room, I could see the bodies of the family members scattered about. There was just a bit of blood and mucus running from the noses of a couple of the victims.

What really caught my eye were the telltale striation patterns on the skin of those victims closest to me.

Uh-oh. I think I know what this is . . .

I realized I needed to get the hell out of there, but before I could take a step, my head exploded with such pain that I nearly went down right where I stood.

It took all the strength I had to fight it off and stumble out the front door and into the yard. My head was spinning.

I went to my knees. Everyone rushed toward me.

"Stay out of the house," I said, fighting off nausea. "It's full of carbon monoxide. That's our killer. Call the city utilities crew and get them to shut off the gas!"

SILENT AND DEADLY

In this investigation, I was the canary in the coal mine. When a Kenda goes down, you know there is something very bad in the air.

Carbon monoxide is an odorless gas that will put you down in a heartbeat. Fumes are produced by your stove, generator, grill, space heater, furnace, or the car warming up with the garage doors shut.

Anything that burns fuel, basically, can create carbon monoxide. If those fumes somehow build up inside a confined area because of a broken or blocked pipe or lack of ventilation, it's good night, Charlie.

You won't smell it, and you won't see it coming. Victims of carbon monoxide poisoning often have a unique skin discoloration in a striated pattern of white and pink. Cops call it "carnation pink and apple-blossom white" as a way to remember it.

Another thing about carbon monoxide poisoning is that the victims suffer severe abdominal pain and think they have to go to the bathroom. That is why one of the kids was found in the bathroom with his pajamas down.

The mother was dressed for bed in a T-shirt and underwear. Like the kids, she probably woke up with her head pounding, made it a few steps into the living room, and was overcome. A planter was knocked over beside her. She probably grabbed it to keep from falling.

The fact that she was overcome so quickly indicated a very high level of carbon monoxide in the house. That was confirmed when the city utility division sent out a guy with a handheld meter. He had to go inside to take a reading.

"Be very careful," I said. "Get in and get out. I was in there only a couple of minutes, and my head is still pounding."

He stepped up on the porch, and the meter's alarm went off.

"Holy shit!" he said, looking back at me. "You weren't kidding."

He opened the door, extended his arm, and put the meter inside.

When he pulled it back out after thirty seconds, the meter showed a concentration one thousand times the strength capable of killing a person.

"I've never seen a reading that high," he said.

We had to purge the deadly gas before we could go back in. The city-owned utility company shut off the natural gas to the home's furnace at the meter. The fire department came out with some giant fans and vented the place.

The ritualistic-murders theory went out the window with the carbon monoxide, so the police brass and the media went home. I wasn't so lucky.

Actually, I didn't want to go home, because something about this case was bothering me. And no, it wasn't the poisonous CO gas still trapped in my thick head, as my wife suggested when notified that I wasn't coming home for a while.

"You can come back home," said my wife. "This isn't a murder investigation. It's a gas leak, so it's accidental."

"I don't know about that," I said. "With concentrations that high, it could be a homicide case. I'm going to keep working a while."

A DEADLY HACK JOB

On January 9, 1990, Sophia Gerardo, thirty-four, moved into a crummy wood-frame rental house with her sons Nash, ten; Mario, thirteen; and Daniel, eight; along with her nephew Mark McPeak, fifteen.

Sophia was fighting for her family's survival when she rented that house. Her husband and her oldest son were in prison, so she was working two jobs and putting in eighty hours a week. One of her jobs was stuffing advertising flyers into the local newspaper.

Desperate for a place to live, she had found the cheapest rental she could afford. They moved in, and on their first night, the kids helped Sophia unpack for several hours before going to sleep in the two small bedrooms.

That was the last anyone heard from them. Over the next few days, family members tried to call Sophia, to check on her and the kids, but couldn't reach her. On the fifth day of no communication, her brother went to the house.

It was a good thing he couldn't get in, or he might have died, too.

The crime lab went to work checking out the source of the heavy carbon monoxide levels in the house. They pulled the grill off the gas-fired wall heater, and it looked as though someone had beaten a part of it with a hammer. No one could identify the part at first, but it appeared that someone had tried to bang it into place.

We brought in a city utilities guy with more expertise. He took one look and said, "Oh, fuck! That's a vent. It's supposed to prevent carbon monoxide from being forced into the home, by venting it out through the roof, but some moron beat it into place to make it fit. The problem is, the part wasn't fitting—because they put the vent in *backwards*."

The knucklehead installation resulted in the "vent" actually turning into a carbon monoxide generator that flooded the house with deadly fumes.

Now the question became, was this just a dumbass mistake? Or was it done with intent to kill? But who would want to kill Sophia and these kids?

We first looked at her husband, who had a lengthy rap sheet, but he'd been locked up for two months. We interviewed other family and friends and learned that Sophia reportedly had not one boyfriend but two.

We checked them out. The dueling boyfriends knew about each other. They tried to implicate each other, but both had alibis, and we let go of that thread.

We found something more promising when our detectives went to City Hall and searched records on the house and its owners. We found that the current owner was Darrell Atkinson, a retired fire captain who was widely known as a slumlord.

He had a bad reputation among the patrol officers who worked in the area. They described him as a bitter old guy who preyed on low-income people, charging them high rents for shitty, poorly maintained houses.

"He complains to us all the time about his renters, but he does nothing to maintain his properties," we were told. "He won't spend a nickel and then raises hell when his tenants complain or bail."

We talked to some of the city firemen who had worked with Atkinson. He wasn't exactly the most popular guy in the firehouse. They said he had grown up dirt poor during the Depression and joined the fire department so he would always have a steady job.

"Mostly, all he would talk about was how much he'd suffered as a child and how he bought up a lot of dumps as rentals because he never wanted to be poor again," one of his former coworkers said.

He had succeeded in becoming one of the city's biggest slumlords and building up a big pile of money, but none of that seemed to relieve his misery. He certainly didn't seem to take any joy in buying himself nice things. Instead, he preyed on the same sort of people who struggled to get by, just as his family had.

While checking those city records, our detectives turned up a very interesting document. It was a city inspection report noting that previous tenants of the same house suffered carbon monoxide poisoning while living there in 1989, just a year before the deaths of Sophia and the four children.

What a coincidence! Or not?

The report said that William Haag and his wife, Becky, were the renters back then. When I read it, I had to laugh at their story, just a little. They put a fresh new spin on the "Not now, honey, I have a headache" excuse.

In the report, Haag said he'd told his wife he had a headache that night before heading to bed. Becky actually suggested that he could either take an aspirin for the headache or have sex with her.

Not surprisingly, Bill passed on the aspirin and took the sex.

The report didn't say, but we'll just assume that afterward they cuddled and fell asleep.

But then it gets even weirder.

Bill and Becky woke up in separate beds—in a hospital.

It wasn't the sex that almost killed them, in case you were wondering.

They got lucky (after getting lucky) when a friend happened by. Normally, that might have been lousy timing, but in this case, it was very fortunate.

The friend knocked and no one answered, but the door was unlocked, so he stepped inside and called out for them.

No answer.

Sensing that something was wrong, he looked into the bedroom and found them unconscious on the floor. He called 911, and the EMTs and ER docs saved their lives by pumping them full of oxygen.

When you breathe in carbon monoxide, it rapidly replaces the oxygen in your bloodstream. At high concentrations like those found in that shitty little house of death, the gas can kill you in just a couple of minutes.

The CDC says that in the United States, at least 430 people die every year from accidental CO poisoning. Another fifty thousand find themselves in the ER due to carbon monoxide intake like the Haags'. Typical symptoms include headaches, dizziness, weakness, nausea, vomiting, chest pain, and confusion.

I highly recommend getting CO detectors for your home. Give them to your friends for Christmas. They save lives. It's a pretty cheap investment, all things considered.

After they learned of the Haags' near-death experience, the city utilities inspectors went out and found that the house had three decrepit wall heaters that were older than dirt. All were tagged as unsafe.

The red tags signaled that no one could occupy the house until the heaters were repaired or replaced by a licensed contractor, then inspected by the city and approved.

We dug into the city files and found that Atkinson simply had shut down two of the faulty wall heaters. There was a note in the file that the city had received notice from the landlord that the third wall heater had been repaired. He included the name of a heating contractor and his phone number.

We brought Atkinson in for questioning on that, and he said it had been repaired. Then he tried to throw in a red herring or two, claiming that Haag might have messed up the vent system by trying to fix it himself after he and his wife nearly died.

It was a typical bullshit attempt to cover his own ass—the old ploy of, "Well, if you don't believe that, how about this?"

We went back to Haag. He said they moved out shortly after being gassed, and he never touched the vent in the crappy wall heater. He did open it up and remove a wad of soot that had built up, because it was stinking up the house.

Our guys also interviewed the contractor about the alleged repair paid for by Atkinson. We showed him the ticket from our public utilities records, featuring his signature, license number, and phone number.

"That's bullshit," he said. "We never went to that house. The landlord called and asked for an estimate. When I told him it would be a hundred dollars for the repair, he hung up on me. I never heard another word from him."

He showed us his service records for the date in question. We believed him. We then described to him the hammered vent put in upside down. He was appalled.

"That's some jackass amateur who didn't know what the hell he was doing," he said. "Our guys would know better."

It appeared that Atkinson had tried to do the repair himself, then filled out the forms claiming that a licensed contractor had done the work. (Because of this case, the city's regulations were tightened up to prevent that sort of deception in the red-tag program.)

Atkinson had faked the signature on the document and lied about the repair, and on top of that, he put the replacement part into the heater backward and then hammered the hell out of it because it wouldn't fit.

Then Atkinson made the house even deadlier. The landlord figured that only one working heater wouldn't keep the entire place warm unless there were no air leaks, so he went around and made sure the house was airtight. That was the one job he actually did right, and it proved fatal for his next renters.

In the process, he turned the heater vent into a lethal weapon, a carbon monoxide death-ray machine. Atkinson had figured they wouldn't complain about it being cold. Of course, they couldn't complain if they were dead, either.

Atkinson claimed that the ancient wall heater had been repaired, but he lied. He was much better at lying than at fixing things.

Keep in mind, it wasn't that he couldn't afford to maintain his properties. He was just cheap. We eventually found out that he had more than a million dollars in the bank, plus all the equity in the many properties he owned.

Greed was the trigger in this homicide case. And believe me, it did become a homicide case. A hardworking woman and four kids were dead because this asshole landlord was too miserly to have the wall heater properly fixed.

The media and police brass lost interest because it happened to a blue-collar family in a poor neighborhood, but I wanted this son of a bitch to pay for what he'd done.

THE LANDLORD FROM HELL

Once we'd built up a good case against him, I paid a visit to the landlord from hell. He lived alone. Not surprising. We sat down in his kitchen for a little chat.

"We have a problem, Mr. Atkinson," I said. "We've found that you lied about having a licensed contractor repair that wall heater after your previous tenants were nearly killed. You did a hack-job repair and then filled out those forms yourself. Then you rented the place to a family of five and they died because of your shitty repair job on your shitty wall heater in your shitty house.

"That sets you up nicely for five counts of criminally negligent homicide, and you are under arrest."

I had expected a denial, an explosion of anger, or at least a plea for mercy. I had no hope for a confession or any sign of remorse. This miser was a cold fish.

His only response was, "What will my bond be?"

I told him probably two hundred thousand, which meant he could post twenty thousand and get out until it was time for his trial.

Hearing that, he stood up from the table, went to a coffee can over his stove, took the lid off, and pulled out a huge wad of hundred-dollar bills. Then he counted out twenty thousand and stuffed the rest back in the coffee can.

"I don't think I did anything wrong," Atkinson said, "but if the court says I did, I'll take my medicine."

"Oh, there will be medicine to take, Mr. Atkinson," I said as I cuffed him, tight as they would go.

Then we drove to the county jail, where he was booked. I didn't stay to watch him walk out. I might have run him over with my squad car, accidentally.

Before he bailed out, I went back to his home to search it after leaving him at the jail. He had elderly friends who kept an eye on him. Atkinson was only seventy-three, but he seemed older than that. Something was off. He just seemed emotionally stunted and lethargic.

There was an older woman there, his friend. Maybe his only friend.

"I arrested him, but he'll probably be back home before long," I told her. "I can't really read him, but he seems depressed, so you might want to keep an eye on him."

"Okay," was all she said. She and Atkinson seemed to have surliness in common.

I really don't know why I cared about his state of mind. Maybe I just wanted to make sure I saw him convicted and locked up for his greed and negligence.

Later, I received word that he had posted bond and gone home. I tried to put the whole case out of my mind and get some R&R with the family that night.

My phone rang at 5:13 a.m.

"Mr. Atkinson was found dead in his car with the engine running in his closed garage," a patrolman said.

He'd killed himself with carbon monoxide. Maybe he figured it was some sort of poetic justice. I found it pathetic, but then, I was glad no one else would die in one of his houses because of his greed.

I went to his house that morning before they cleared it for release of his body. He was slumped behind the wheel; his skin was clearly marked by the "carnation pink and apple-blossom white" striations characteristic of CO poisoning.

Despite my contempt for Atkinson, I was starting to feel a little sad for him when his neighbor-lady friend walked up to me, looking as if she wanted to strangle me with her old-lady shawl.

"You pulled the trigger on him!" she shrieked.

Then she kicked me so hard in the shin, I damn near went down. If the Broncos ever needed a punter, I'd recommend that old biddy to them. She had a leg on her.

She was still cussing at me as two patrolmen dragged her away. They were going to arrest her for assaulting a police officer, but I told them to let her go.

I left her bawling in the driveway. Then I went to the nearest 7-Eleven store and bought a box of Band-Aids because the blood was seeping through my pants and down my leg. I did my own first aid on a curb outside the store.

Then I went back inside the 7-Eleven and did something I hadn't done for three years. I bought a pack of Marlboros, went back to my unmarked car, and smoked every one of them—with the windows down, just in case.

Smoking can kill a guy, you know.

Then my radio went off with another homicide report, and I got right back into the game.

AND THEN THIS HAPPENED . . .

Fast-forward twenty years. By then I'm long retired from the police department and working with a camera crew in Denver, on a commercial for *Homicide Hunter*.

The idea of the commercial was built around me doing a murder investigation. We were shooting in an alley in a really shitty part of downtown because they wanted it to look gritty and realistic. We were doing the shoot at two a.m. to avoid a lot of traffic and gawkers.

The commercial producers had hired six off-duty Denver cops as security on the set. There was one older guy and a few younger cops. Before we started shooting, they all came up to say they liked the show. We stood there just shooting the breeze while waiting for the cameras and lighting to be set up.

The older cop was a guy named Mendez. I teased him saying that I was surprised to see a veteran out pulling security for extra cash, which was usually something younger guys with families did.

"Oh, Joe, when I heard you were going to be here, I had to come down," he said. "I had a family reunion a while back, and when I told my cousin you were coming to Denver, he asked me to get a photograph with you."

I said I'd be glad to do that.

"Is your cousin a fan of the show?" I asked, just making small talk.

"Well, yeah," said Officer Mendez, "but that's not the reason you're his hero."

"Why would I be his hero?" I asked.

"Well, do you remember the Gerardo case, where the woman and four kids died of carbon monoxide poisoning in a rental house?"

"Sure I do. That case was a heartbreaker," I said.

"My cousin's son was best friends with the ten-year-old Gerardo boy. My cousin's boy was invited to stay all night with him on the night they all died, but his mother wouldn't let him go, because he was sick.

"He's never gotten over the fact that his friend died that night," Mendez said. "He and his family consider you a hero for figuring out what happened and charging that landlord."

I told him I was glad to help bring him some peace over the loss of his friend.

Hearing his story gave me a little peace, too. Just a little, but I'll take what I can get.

CHAPTER SIX:
MURDER IN A MOM 'N' POP SHOP

THE TRIGGER: MONEY

This case still gets to me, so as I tell it, you may have to excuse me if I need to go outside and sledgehammer a dirt mound or just scream into my palms until drool drips from my fingers.

I was just a year into my job as a homicide detective in November 1978 when the call came in. One dead, another close to it, at a neighborhood grocery on the poor side of town.

I'd been doing search warrant–paperwork training with my brand-spanking-new partner, Manny, a smart kid who would later become a respected police chief in a nearby town.

At that point, he had just moved over from patrol and had never worked a homicide.

"Here is your golden opportunity," I said. "Mount up."

Upon arrival at the chaotic crime scene, Manny went from the new guy to an old guy in about thirty minutes.

This job will do that to you.

The eighty-three-year-old guy who owned the mom-and-pop

grocery was facedown on the floor in a halo of blood. He had multiple stab wounds, and it looked as if someone had stomped all over his lower body. He was breathing when the EMTs arrived, but died while they were treating him.

Paramedics were preparing to evacuate his wife to the ER. They had found her under a coffee table. She probably crawled there to escape whoever had stabbed and kicked her. Rosa Melena was still breathing, but it didn't look as though she'd make it. Her face appeared to be crushed on one side. Blood was dripping from her ear.

They were found in their tiny apartment carved out of the back of the store, which was just through the living-room door. The grocery's cash register drawer was open, and a coin tray was on the floor. There was a penny on the floor; other than that, the register was empty.

It was sad, pathetic, and disturbing. There probably wasn't two hundred dollars in inventory in the whole place. Maybe ten one-gallon containers of milk and fifteen loaves of bread.

They had scraped by for forty-one years and never had any trouble. They were heroes to many in the neighborhood, providing food to families in need. For this to happen to them was just tragic.

The couple's adult son, Rudy, was there when we arrived. He also worked in the store but had gone to his house next door for lunch with his wife. He had rushed over after seeing a man and a woman running from his parents' place and down the alley behind their houses.

Rudy, who was in his sixties, said he had tried to give his father CPR after calling 911. He was badly shaken, his shoulders heaving with sobs.

I felt bad, but I had to keep asking questions.

"I'm sorry, can you tell me how much money was in the cash drawer?"

"Thirty-two dollars and change," he said.

Then he looked at me, tears flowing down his face, walked up to me, and put an arm around me.

"Please find the guy who killed my dad," he said.

"I will, and I will lock him up," I said.

And I did.

GOOD SAMARITANS BROUGHT DOWN

Severino "Sam" Melena and his wife, Rosa, seventy-three, were good people in a bad part of town. Sam had originally migrated illegally from Mexico to Colorado to take a job in the silver mines in Georgetown. He had also mined coal, I believe. Sam was just a hardworking man who had also worked on the railroad, in a steel mill, and as a rancher.

I identified with him in part because I grew up in a coal-mining family in Pennsylvania and I knew just what he'd had to go through to support his family. His son shared some stories with me, and my mind took me back to childhood memories of family members talking about cave-ins and poisonous gases. My grandfather was killed in a coal-mining accident. My great uncle, father, and uncle all worked in the mines.

My path to the police department was partly the result of my determination not to live like a mole underground, waiting to be crushed or gassed. It tore at my heart that Sam Melena had survived that difficult life and then been killed for a few dollars.

Once he and his family moved to Colorado Springs, they rented their building from a woman who owned a bunch of seedy properties built during the war. The landlady was sort of a benevolent matriarch for the down-and-out residents of the area.

She gave the Melenas a rent discount for operating the little grocery to provide milk and bread and other basics to neighborhood folks who couldn't afford cars or bus fare.

The Melenas were the salt of the earth, just the nicest people. In his later years, Sam taught music and English lessons to other Latinos at the local YMCA. Their son, Rudy, was a great guy, too. He served on the local housing board and was an advocate for the working-class and poor Latinos who lived in the area.

Many of them, like Sam and Rosa, were not legal residents of the United States, but they were assets to their community. The family was known for their kindness and concern for others. If you had no cash for groceries, no problem. Take care of it when you get paid.

Back in the 1950s and '60s, most cities and towns had small corner groceries in neighborhoods. Parents could send their kids over to pick up a couple of cans of soup or some hamburger meat. They'd just say, "Charge it to our ticket."

The grocer would send a weekly or monthly bill, and families paid up. There was more trust back then. The grocery owner usually lived in the back of the store, so you were neighbors, too.

Those stores began to fade in the 1970s as the big national chains like IGA and Piggly Wiggly moved into towns, offering lower prices and a bigger selection. They didn't take credit. They weren't your neighbor. They didn't trust you to pay later.

"Dad never lost money doing that," Rudy told me. "People might have taken a while, but they always came back and paid him because he was so good to them."

Good people—a rarity in my world. Maybe in yours, too.

Unfortunately, we have way too many dirtbags like Lawrence Eugene Todd, nineteen, who was quickly identified as a suspect in this case. Rudy had spotted him and his very easy-to-spot girlfriend running down the alley while Rudy was eating lunch next door.

He knew them because he'd helped the ragged couple find a place to stay down the street. They had shown up at the store a few weeks earlier, saying they were homeless and without money, begging for help.

When we talked to Rudy that day at the store, he said the couple might have fled to that apartment, but we sent our guys over and they had cleared out. They were in the wind.

I knew they wouldn't be that hard to find. They weren't Bonnie and Clyde—more like the doofus pair from *Dumb and Dumber.*

KILLER COUPLE

Lawrence Eugene Todd was a blood-sucking leech on the neighborhood, if not a running sore on the face of the planet. He was officially a soldier in the US Army, but he'd given himself leave after deciding he wasn't cut out for the rigors of military life.

Besides, he had a girlfriend, Vicki, who was a major distraction from his military duties. She was distracting, period. Vicki was nearly six feet tall, with natural bright-red hair, a frizzy white-girl Afro, and a million freckles.

We learned that she never completed grade school and spent most of her teen years as a runaway labeled "out of control." At least, she was never hard to find. With her flaming, flopping hair adding to her considerable height, Vicki stood out in any crowd.

She was not unattractive, but she had an IQ lower than sea level, and she was a magnet for lowlifes and losers. Lawrence and Vicki were an interracial couple, and they had claimed they were outcasts in our fair state. So they decided to move to central California, where they'd first met. We later found out that Lawrence came from a long line of criminals.

The California cops told reporters his family was "notorious." Lawrence Todd had a criminal record dating back at least five years, with multiple juvenile convictions, and charges ranging from assault with a deadly to burglary and resisting arrest. According to media reports, just a couple of years before his savage attack on the Melenas, two of Todd's brothers were convicted for a home burglary that turned into a murder when the homeowner they had tied up and gagged died of suffocation.

Maybe Lawrence had joined the army to get away from bad influences at home, but he seemed to bring all that baggage with him. The military life certainly didn't help him get straight.

"Fuck the army" was Lawrence's go-to response when reminded of his commitment to our nation's defense. He was not a patriot, nor much of a human.

As you might imagine, his rebellious attitude did not go over well with his commanding officers or with his comrades in arms, so Lawrence had fled Fort Carson for civilian accommodations in Colorado Springs.

He and Vicki needed a pad as a home base before launching Lawrence's AWOL plan. They had no money, but when they first showed up at Melena's grocery, Rudy had helped them out, much to his later regret.

Finding shelter solved one problem for the sketchy couple. They had a roof over their heads for a few nights, but they still had no money. And they needed cash to get out of Dodge and make their way to La-La Land, where Lawrence figured he could reconnect with his criminal past and never again have to wear camouflage or pull KP duty.

Maybe that's unfair. He might have been dreaming of becoming a reality TV show star. *Assholes Who Go AWOL* is one possible series title. (I came up with that on my own, by the way.)

At any rate, Lawrence and Vicki devised their own GoFundMe plan for raising the loot they needed to hotfoot it out of Colorado Springs. Once they moved into the Melenas' neighborhood, they began preying on everyone around them. Just five hours before the grocery store attack was reported, the woman who lived in an apartment above the couple reported that sixty-five dollars in food stamps had been stolen.

Vicki had tried to cash in the neighbor's food stamps at Melena's store earlier. When the neighbor confronted her, she gave back eleven dollars' worth of the stamps. Others in the neighborhood said the predatory couple often went door-to-door in their bare feet, begging for food, cigarettes, or money.

When mooching didn't work, Lawrence and his gal pal turned to what they knew best: bloodthirsty crime. They decided to rob the very family who had shown them nothing but kindness and compassion.

If you've ever wondered why I tend to prefer the company of slobbering dogs and probably even rabid wolves over my fellow humans, I offer up this predatory pair as evidence in aggravation and mitigation.

Our simpleton couple devised a simpleton's plan to steal whatever meager funds were in the Melenas' cash register and then run off to California to live happily ever after, like the Kardashians . . . or the Manson family.

After trolling the neighborhood, begging money from strangers for a couple of days without success, Lawrence and Vicki entered the grocery store and asked Sam if they could use his telephone.

This was back when dinosaurs roamed the earth and there were no smartphones. Not that these two dunces could have qualified to own one anyway.

Everyone in the neighborhood knew that Sam would let them use his telephone for local calls. He charged only a quarter for this service. They also knew that Sam had to go back into his apartment and bring out the phone, which had an extra-long cord so they could use it in both the store and their home.

Lawrence's feeble plan was to have Vicki raid the cash register while he followed Sam to the back. But he didn't stick with the plan. Instead, he followed the old guy and savagely attacked him and his wife while Vicki cleared out the cash register.

They then ran out the back of the store and down the alley, where Rudy spotted them from his kitchen window. He ran to check on his parents and found them near death.

As I said, this case bothered the hell out of me, and it still does. It was a horrible, senseless, brutal crime. The local media didn't pay much attention to the Melena murder-and-beating case, because it was a poor neighborhood. That pissed me off, too.

And it made me all the more determined to bring this monstrous couple to justice.

WORKING THE CASE

We put out a blast broadcast to all law enforcement in the country that Lawrence and Vicki were wanted for the Melena murder. In the meantime, we searched for witnesses and any information we could gather on the suspects.

We had to wait a couple of days before her doctors would let us talk to Mrs. Melena, who surprised everyone by hanging on to life. I always tried to put on my emotional body armor when interviewing victims, especially those who had lost loved ones. I hoped wrapping Kevlar panels around my heart would keep me from losing it.

Every now and then, though, a dagger slipped through.

Rosa hit me hard.

We talked to her doctor first, in the hallway outside her room. I could see Rosa, a tiny, frail woman bruised and bandaged from head to toe, as he filled us in on her condition.

"Mrs. Melena has several broken bones, and a knife laceration in her chest," her doctor said. "But the blade hit a bone, so it didn't do as much damage as we feared at first. She will likely survive this because she's in such good health otherwise. You can talk to her, but keep it brief, please."

"One more thing," the doctor said quietly. "We haven't told her that her husband died. She's not ready for that yet."

Oh, man, that made our talk more difficult because it was a big secret to guard.

We walked into her room. Rosa had her head on the pillow, and the right side of her face was unmarked. She was sleeping. The nurse gently touched her shoulder to awaken her.

"These detectives would like to talk with you, Rosa. They are trying to find the person who hurt you."

Rosa was more comfortable speaking Spanish. My young partner, Manny, was Puerto Rican and bilingual, so he spoke to her softly.

She turned to look at him, changing position, and for the first time we saw the extent of the damage to the left side of her face.

I had to stifle my anger. You could clearly make out the imprint of a sneaker sole where Lawrence Todd had stomped on her cheek.

Manny and I were shocked at the sight of that. He must have been trying to crush her face. We photographed the injury as Rosa described the attack.

She knew the couple by name. They had asked to use the phone. Sam went back to the apartment to get it. Lawrence followed him. He attacked them with a five-inch Buck knife, stabbing them, knocking them to the floor, and then stomping on them.

He kept kicking them even after they couldn't move, as Vicki grabbed what little there was in the store's cash register.

After giving her account in halting Spanish, Rosa looked up at us and said, "What about my Sam?"

Oh, damn, I can't answer that, I thought.

I said, "Mrs. Melena, we will find the people who hurt your Sam, and we will make sure they pay for it."

Then Manny and I got out of there before we both lost it.

FIENDS IN FLIGHT

Lawrence and Vicki had managed to hitch a ride to Denver with a trucker. The trucker told us later that he'd picked them up even though the idiot noticed blood on Todd's jacket.

"Not very smart," I said. "You were lucky he didn't slice and dice you and steal your semi and all its contents."

He had dropped them off at a truck stop near the intersection known as the Mousetrap, where the major interstates 70 and 25 intersect just north of downtown Denver.

I don't know what it was about this couple. Even though they were vicious scum, they attracted do-gooders everywhere they went. They were panhandling outside the truck stop when a Christian couple with kids in the car offered to take the strangers to their nearby home, feed them, and let them stay the night.

Good Lord, Good Samaritans! You have to be more selective than that! Sure, be kind if you must, but be smart, too! Think about your kids! Do what's right for them and their safety before picking up dirtbag strangers at truck stops.

Sure, you have faith and you believe in your Lord and Savior, but what if the Big Guy is busy that night protecting other souls in Ireland or Kosovo? You've got to watch out for your own.

I'm not being dramatic. We learned later that while in the Denver couple's home, sleeping in their guest bedroom, Lawrence told Vicki that he wanted to kill their entire host family, steal whatever they could find, then take their car.

There was only one problem with his plan, Lawrence said.

"I only have a knife," he told his girlfriend. "If I had a gun, I could probably do it."

While the family slept, their killer guest searched the house for a suitable weapon but couldn't find one, so he gave up on that plan.

Even a murdering son of a bitch has to know his limitations.

They all had a lovely breakfast the next morning. I'm sure they said grace, blessed their bagels, and exchanged pleasantries. Then the clueless Christians drove them back out to the truck stop and dropped them off.

Another trucker picked them up and headed West on I-70. They made it 350 miles and into the loneliest reaches of the state of Utah before the trucker had to fuel up at Crescent Junction, about four hundred miles due west of Colorado Springs.

It was his lucky day. Lawrence was probably sizing him up for a stabbing, too. But a woman at this truck stop was an avid fan of law enforcement. I'd wager she never missed an episode of *Barney Miller, Kojak, The Rockford Files, Hawaii Five-O,* or *Police Woman.*

Especially *Police Woman.*

Let's call her Cagney Ann Lacey, just for fun. Her hobby was listening to police scanners and monitoring law enforcement bulletins.

Our cop groupie Cagney dreamed of one day spotting a bad guy and calling in the good guys. She desperately wanted to play the hero. Bless her little heart.

She was primed and ready, alert and sharp-eyed, with her fingers poised over the dial.

And on that particular day, her wildest *Starsky & Hutch* fantasies came true when into her truck stop walked two of the most wanted fugitives of the day: a short, stocky Black male with a flashy, trashy long-legged white girl sporting a red frizz 'fro.

She no doubt noted that they looked a little like the Mod Squad, minus the white guy. For our law enforcement fangirl, this was like a double-scoop sundae with a giant cherry on the top.

But our Cagney was cagey. She didn't want to see the truck stop shot up, so she watched and waited as Lawrence and Vicki used the restrooms and bought some snacks, while their trucker filled up the fuel tanks.

As soon as they hopped back in the cab and drove off, Cagney ran to the phone and punched out 9-1-1 faster than Marshall Dillon could slap leather.

She gave an absolutely perfect description of the vehicle, its license plate number, the trucker, and his two passengers. The Utah Highway Patrol was promptly dispatched to make a felony stop on two fugitives wanted in a Colorado Springs homicide.

The Utah Highway Patrol officers made it look like a routine weight-check stop when they pulled over the eighteen-wheeler. Once they had him stopped, though, they produced a bullhorn and their firearms, ordering the trucker and his passengers out of the cab with their hands up.

There was no resistance and, this being eastern Utah, nowhere to run.

The highway patrol officers informed Lawrence and Vicki that they were under arrest for murder and aggravated assault, among other things.

They then uncuffed the trucker and informed him that he was one lucky son of a bitch because he was still alive and breathing.

"I ain't never gonna pick up hitchhikers anymore," he told local reporters.

Some people are slow learners, but they finally get it when they escape death. Or not.

EXTRADITION JOYRIDE

I got the call that the killers of Sam Melena were in custody in Utah out in the middle of nowhere.

"Manny, my friend, go home, pack your bags with enough clothing for five days, and meet me at the airport in an hour," I said to my partner. "We're bringing those two assholes back for trial."

Manny had a wife who had just returned to work after having a baby six weeks earlier. He hesitated because he was supposed to finish his shift, go home, and relieve the babysitter while his wife continued her shift.

"But my wife isn't home yet, Joe," he said.

"But, Manny, she isn't going with us," I replied. "It's just you and me. I'll have my wife call Judy and work it out. You are a big-boy detective now, and duty calls us to the Beehive State, home of the Mormon Tabernacle Choir and all five hundred members of the Osmond Family."

We flew into Salt Lake City that Friday night and then drove south two hours to the Carbon County Jail in Price, Utah, population just over seven thousand if you count all the dinosaur bones in their Prehistoric Museum.

We hit town too late to visit the jail, so we booked a room in a no-tell motel. No Ritz Carlton for us, even if there had been one within 150 miles. The Colorado Springs Police Department had a slim travel budget. We were lucky they didn't make us spend the night under a viaduct.

"We're getting up at four so we can get this show on the road," I told Manny as I tucked him in for the night.

"In the morning?" he replied.

"Yeah, in the morning. We have to make a ten a.m. flight in Salt Lake City."

About five hours later, I was up and at 'em as planned.

Manny was sleeping like a fucking stone.

I thought he was dead. He didn't move when I told him to wake up. He didn't move when I poked his shoulder or flicked his ear.

So I grabbed him and shook him.

Still nothing.

He left me no choice.

I reached down, gripped the steel legs of the bed, and turned it over with Detective Sleeping Beauty on board.

Manny came up out of his dead sleep with his nine-millimeter in his hand, ready to put a slug between my eyes.

Impressive autoresponse!

"Are you awake now, you SOB?" I said.

"Damn you, Kenda!" Then he laughed, a little.

We grabbed our suitcases and headed for the local hoosegow before the sun came up.

It was Saturday, and we hit a snag when we tried to check out the diabolical duo.

Frizzy-headed Vicki was all gung ho to go back to Colorado with us— even to face a first-degree murder charge—because, as she exclaimed, "I've never flown in no plane before!"

Lawrence, on the other hand, was playing hard to get. No stranger to the world of criminal law, he refused consent to go with us, forcing an extradition hearing.

Naturally, the county courthouse is closed on Saturdays, so we had to find a friendly judge, or at least one with a few minutes to spare before heading out to his favorite trout stream.

"We gotta make this fast because the judge wants to go fishin'," said the bailiff.

"All rise, court is in session!"

In walked our judge, wearing the traditional black robe as well as a fishing hat with flies and lures sticking out of it.

Judge Trout Stalker looked at our noncompliant suspect and said, "Are you Lawrence Todd?"

Lawrence nodded in the affirmative.

"Extradition granted! Court closed!"

And then the judge headed for a babbling brook.

We didn't want to haul both of them back at the same time, because Lawrence was a handful. So we put him on ice at the county jail, with plans for Manny to return a few days later and escort him with some assistance from federal marshals.

So it was just Manny, Vicki, and me who boarded on that trip. Vicki was like a kid in an amusement park at the airport. She was peeing herself about her first plane trip, despite the handcuffs and criminal charges. Actually, I'm not sure the ditzy kid had a clue to what was waiting for her in Colorado. She seemed incapable of thinking more than five minutes ahead.

When we perform extraditions on commercial flights, the protocol is to let us take our prisoners onto the plane before any other passengers. They don't want to scare the law-abiding citizens on board.

I had a London Fog raincoat that I draped over Vicki's handcuffs. Manny and I walked her down the ramp and into the plane. We put her in a seat between us.

We had just settled in for the ride when a flight attendant comes up, grabs the raincoat, and says, "Let me hang this up for you."

She yanked it away, exposing the handcuffs on our Little Orphan Annie look-alike.

Manny looked up into the flight attendant's startled face and delivered a deadpan line: "My partner here is into bondage."

The flight attendant looked as if she might jump out of the plane.

"Can I have my coat back, please?" I said, showing her my badge.

Even as I covered up her handcuffs, Vicki was oblivious.

"Flying is so much fun!" she squealed.

KENDA FOR THE PROSECUTION

I'm not a lawyer on TV, but sometimes I play one in the courtroom. Actually, in this case, the prosecutor asked me to sit next to him as an advisory witness. They do this from time to time when it's a complicated case.

The district attorney figures the detective who ran the investigation knows it inside and out and can catch any lies that the defendants or their lawyers try to pass as truth.

Lawrence Todd was our only defendant because Vicki copped a plea after agreeing to testify against him. Love has its limits, you know. Especially when one of the lovers did the actual killing and the other doesn't want to pay the price for the murder.

I was glad to have Vicki on our team, even though she was an idiot. Or maybe because she was *our* idiot by then. She smiled all the way on the flight home and during our interrogations and interviews, not to mention the trial.

While questioning her about meeting Lawrence in California in their early days, I asked her where she'd lived in LA.

"In a yellow house," she said.

"Thanks for narrowing it down," I replied.

She didn't know her address. I'd be surprised if she knew her own birth date. I don't know how she made it out to Colorado on her own. She said she took a bus, which probably stopped just a thousand times on its way to Colorado Springs.

Vicki had no brains and no filter. She may have been incapable of lying. She would just blurt out the truth. This is what we good guys like to call "damning testimony."

I advised the prosecutor of Vicki's childlike ways and fed him questions to throw at her, based on all that she had shared with me in our conversations at the county jail after her arrest.

I'm sure Lawrence Todd does not recall her testimony as fondly as I do, but fuck him.

With Vicki on the stand, blissfully sharing her account of the horrendous attack on the Melenas, I tugged on the prosecutor's sports coat and said, "Ask her what Lawrence said when he stomped on Sam Melena's legs after stabbing him."

The prosecutor gladly put the question to Vicki, who chirped, "Oh, yeah, Larry said that he wanted to hear his bones break."

The entire jury turned and glared knives and bullets at Lawrence. Talk about a group death stare. There was a split second of shocked silence, and then the courtroom went up for grabs. It was pandemonium.

There was a large contingent from the Melena family, and even more friends and neighbors, and they went berserk, trying to crawl over the gates to get to Lawrence Todd, screaming and cursing him in at least four languages.

"Bailiff, order in the court! Bailiffs, order in the court!"

The judge had to threaten to clear the courtroom before the crowd settled down.

Thank you, Miss Vicki.

The defense attorneys waved the surrender flag, threw in the towel, and probably planned their retirement in that moment.

"No questions, Your Honor."

The defense wanted her off the stand before she got them *all* sent to prison.

I turned to the DA and said, "Trial over. Get out the rope."

Of course, there was still the formality of sending the jury in for deliberations. That took all of five minutes. They even skipped their free meal, which is rare.

The jurors basically did a line dance into the deliberation room and right back out.

Guilty on all charges.

The trigger in this case was evil. It wasn't a crime of greed or jealousy or passion or revenge. It was plain evil at work.

The judge sentenced the guilty bastard to life in prison for murdering Sam Melena and threw in twenty to thirty years for armed robbery, up to eight years for conspiracy, and a year for third-degree assault.

Personally, I would have recommend dragging his ass into the courthouse square, stabbing him, stomping him, shooting him in the forehead, and then hanging him.

But that's why I'm not a judge.

May you rot in hell, Lawrence Todd.

CHAPTER SEVEN:
A NEST OF VIPERS

THE TRIGGER: REVENGE, RAGE, AND MONEY

Multiple shots fired in the apartment complex at 2100 Preuss Road on the South Side.

A barrage of 911 calls lit up the operations center at the Colorado Springs Police Department just before one thirty a.m. on July 15, 1991.

Our patrol officers were dispatched. They arrived to find alarmed residents shouting and weeping in doorways and outside the four drab two-story buildings.

The low-rent complex was well known to our department as a nest of vipers, swarming with gangbangers, drug dealers, sex workers, and other bad actors. Not everyone who lived there was a criminal, but everyone who lived there had criminals for neighbors.

Our guys had just arrived when another call came into the 911 operations center, this one from nearby St. Francis Hospital's emergency room. They had a twenty-two-year-old woman, Sharon Coleman, with a severe gunshot wound. Her boyfriend had brought her in, saying she was shot in his car as they were leaving the parking lot at 2100 Preuss Road.

It was going to be a long night, and an even longer investigation. This was our nineteenth homicide of the year, and the third in three days. The South Side had become a shooting gallery.

While the ER docs were struggling to stop the young woman's massive bleeding, our patrol officers went to the hospital, picked up the nineteen-year-old boyfriend, Ernest "Sonny" Wright III, and brought him back to the apartment complex to try to figure out what had happened.

They learned he'd been dating Coleman for two years. She was a churchgoing young woman who worked at Hamburger Haven and Taco Bell. She had worked that night, so she couldn't go to a party with him. After getting off, she had gone to visit his mother in the complex.

Sonny had picked her up there after leaving the party. They were driving out of the parking lot when he saw a muzzle flash come from neighboring Adams Park. Then he heard a shot, and something hit his car.

Sharon Coleman moaned in the seat next to him. Wright saw a rapidly growing bloodstain on her blouse, so he drove as fast as he could to St. Francis Hospital.

As the patrol officers were interviewing Wright, dispatch called and said the ER doctors had lost their ninety-minute fight to save Sharon Coleman.

She never knew what hit her that night.

They say life is random. Death has it beat.

FIELD OF FIRE

The death of Sharon Coleman shifted the shooting investigation to a homicide investigation. I was the lieutenant commander in charge of major crimes, including homicide. I got the call while nestled all snug in my bed.

I drove to the south side in my unmarked car and walked into a chaotic scene, as usual. Welcome to the world of murder and mayhem.

Residents were crying, frantic and scared, which was understandable given that a rapid explosion of high-caliber, high-velocity gunfire had ripped through their buildings and vehicles.

Even in this rough part of town, that level of violence was rare.

The real mystery was how more people weren't killed or maimed in this rampage. There weren't many windows in these buildings, but a lot of them were shattered.

We found bullet holes in walls and in at least three vehicles. Residents ran up to us, reporting muzzle flashes from a park across the street. Some had heard bullets whizzing by their beds.

Several said they had seen a group of men and women arguing in the parking lot just before the shootings. We had reports of two cars leaving the area at high speed after the shooting.

In talking to residents, our guys were amazed we didn't have at least ten shooting victims instead of one. A young father said he was in his apartment and heard gunfire, then screams from his four- and seven-year-old daughters. When he ran to their bedroom, he saw smoke that appeared to be coming from a hole in a metal closet door. He found an expended round on the bed beside the youngest girl, who said she had felt something burn her leg.

Another parent found a bullet lodged in a wall just above her child's bed. The child had been sleeping in it at the time of the shootings.

A woman resident showed us where a bullet had entered her apartment through an outside wall just six inches above the floor, then penetrated the mattress she was sleeping on, just inches below her, and exited from the end of it.

Yet another resident found fragments of a bullet in the pocket of her blue jeans—in her closet. The bullet had ricocheted off a dozen other points in the apartment before landing there. We eventually counted at least fifteen rounds after a sweep of the area by a local treasure-hunting club armed with their metal detectors.

When our officers reported all this back to me, my first thought wasn't about finding any suspects—it was about making sure there weren't more victims.

"We need to account right away for everyone who lives in these buildings," I said.

We obtained a list of all residents from the manager. Then we organized a physical search, knocking on doors, checking for other dead or wounded, and also looking for any suspects who might be hiding out, waiting for the smoke to clear.

Is this your apartment? If not, where do you live?

Of course, in this world, nobody *lives* anywhere. They *stay.* As in "I stay here sometimes. Other times, I stay somewheres else."

Going door to door in an unstable shithole environment like that is dangerous, nerve-racking work. You never know who will open the door, who will be hiding in the closet or under the bed. (Yes, they really do hide there in real life.)

Guns are everywhere, so you have to be prepared to defend yourself at all times. Alcohol and drugs make the door-to-door search even more volatile. You might wake up a drunk-ass idiot or some drugged-out, methed-up maniac who knows there is a ten-year-old outstanding warrant with his name on it.

Guilty or innocent, it's not unusual for someone to go ballistic and berserk in these situations. It's happened many times, believe me.

But hey, it's part of the job, and we did it that night and many others while praying that we would wake up the next morning staring at something other than a death shroud at the coroner's office, or the inside of a hospital sheet.

Fortunately, we didn't find any more victims, which amazed even a hard-nosed veteran detective like me. That night, bullets were flying everywhere at supersonic speeds. We kept finding more bullet holes in buildings and parked cars.

We also learned that on the night before this shooting, dozens of shots from a variety of weapons were fired into the parked vehicle of a resident who just happened to be the aunt of Sonny Wright.

We found that very interesting but also complicating. Was it a coincidence, or part of an attempt to kill or frighten Sonny and his family?

BOYFRIEND OR FOE?

When our guys asked Sonny if someone might have been trying to kill him, he had no problem coming up with several potential candidates. It seems our young friend was a player entangled in nearly every illicit game in the apartment complex.

He'd been released from prison just two months earlier after serving about five months for violating his probation on a car-theft charge. Sonny also admitted that he had bought crack from dealers living there. He had also danced in and out of favor with several Crips gang members and their affiliated "Cripettes."

Their name may sound like a rougher version of Destiny's Child, but this girl band didn't make music. They were gang groupies.

One of their associates was a lovely lass named Peaches, whom Sonny casually described as "my other girlfriend." She was only seventeen and still in high school. Sonny, two years her senior, apparently had wooed and won her.

But alas, Peaches turned sour.

Just two weeks earlier, she had confronted Sonny, claiming she was pregnant with his child. She then demanded that he drop Sharon and see only her.

Since Peaches made her demands while waving a gun in one hand and a heavy chair leg in the other, Sonny took her seriously. She also threatened to kill Sharon, who happened to show up during her tirade.

(As a student of violence, I found this an interesting choice of weaponry. Why did she need the chair leg if she had a gun? Did she plan on shooting him and then bashing him with the piece of furniture? Or was she intent on bashing him and then shooting him? So many questions, but I digress. Back to Sonny and his list of potential assassins.)

I was about to note that hell hath no fury like Peaches scorned when Sonny offered, with no little pride, that she was not the only pissed-off female threatening his health and welfare.

He explained that on the Fourth of July, just eleven days before Coleman's murder, he had an altercation with three Cripettes who frequented an apartment above his mother's.

One of them, known as "China Doll," lit a firecracker and threw it at his car as he drove by. Unpleasantries were exchanged.

China Doll then introduced a handgun to the conversation and fired several shots into the air. Sonny, who seemed to have a knack for inciting females with firearms, wisely left the scene.

He confided to us that China Doll might hold a grudge against him still. We made a note to track down this new potential suspect. And then, just for good measure, Sonny threw out one more potential foe.

A male known as "Crow." Sonny said Crow accused him of stealing a gun, which Sonny denied. Still, once again, Sonny thought Crow might want him dead.

I made a mental note not to stand too close to Sonny in public.

A TANGLED WEB TO UNWEAVE

So, we had one homicide victim and a lot of bullet holes, likely from an AK-47, the weapon of choice for homicidal maniacs around the world.

The obvious question we ask in every murder case is, "Who benefits from this victim's death?" Did killing Sharon Coleman satisfy someone's desire for revenge? With money? With one less romantic rival?

Our list of suspects included Sonny and his many enemies, most of whom were gang members, gang groupies, or gang wannabes known only by their street monikers like Peaches, China Doll, Sea Dog, and, my personal favorite, Shitty Moe.

Historically, Colorado Springs gangbangers were rarely affiliated with major city gangs. The entrenched urban gangs often were powerful, decades-old criminal enterprises with a well-defined hierarchy that had strict rules and strong-arm enforcement tactics.

Until the early 1990s, most of our local gang members were nitwits— mere poseurs, pretenders, and petty criminals—although that didn't make them any less dangerous. Wannabe gang members tend to overcompensate for their lack of true street cred with extreme violence and unpredictable patterns of behavior. Many act out to make a name for themselves. Many more are running scared. They don't have the discipline that is enforced with real gangs.

Urban gang members kill only under orders sent down by their bosses, who are older, more averse to prison time, and making a lot of money that they don't want to lose. Rarely do street-level gang members randomly murder anyone who isn't in a competing gang, isn't a traitor to the gang, or doesn't somehow pose a threat to the gang's income.

While the majority of our gang members were not affiliated with the big national criminal organizations, we were finding that gangs from LA and other major cities were setting up "franchises" to run drugs and guns in our area. They were recruiting from the wannabe local yokels to do their dirty work.

The arrival of these more disciplined LA gang members had brought more violence because they were not shy about shooting anyone who stood in the way of their efforts to expand their drug markets in our area. This helped explain why 1991 was such a busy year for my homicide squad. And we weren't the only cops working overtime.

SO MANY CRIMES, SO LITTLE TIME

Let me take you behind the blue curtain that surrounded this investigation from the get-go. This case was a bit more complex than most because at least two or three other investigations were already underway in that same apartment complex on the night that Sharon Coleman died.

Many of the people living and hanging out at the apartment complex were also suspects or witnesses tied to two murders on the south side the two previous nights. One theory was that the shooting that killed Coleman was a retaliation for one or both of those previous homicides.

There were also ongoing gang, drug-dealing, and gun-running investigations focused on many of the same players living or hanging out in the apartment complex.

We had a bunch of cops staring into the same cesspool of more than a hundred suspects living in that complex. Between our homicide detectives, the narcotics squad, and the gangbusters focused on the area, we had to be careful not to trip over each other, or at least not to mess up each other's investigations.

Over the next four months, we worked together, trading information and also sharing informants. But we always had to be careful that they weren't just repeating rumors or suspicions that spread like a virus in the underworld. Informants are usually addicts looking to trade information for cash or to stay out of jail. So it's always a game with them.

One of my favorite tactics was to search them and take away all their Bic lighters. They needed them to smoke crack, and they were tough to come by in that world. You'd be surprised how much information you'd get out of a crackhead if you flicked his Bic.

Still, sorting out all the players, their street names, and the rumors and false information in this case proved difficult. Sonny's own criminal activities made him an unreliable witness, as well as a suspect. For example, we spent a lot of time trying to figure out why someone shot up his aunt's car the night before Sharon Coleman was killed. We wondered whether the two events were connected.

However, we eventually figured out that Sonny's aunt had a car of the same model and color as one that belonged to a noted gangbanger who lived in the same complex. His enemies meant to shoot up his car but targeted the aunt's wheels by mistake. They totally aerated it with ammo. If the aunt's car had been drivable, it would have whistled up a symphony.

But it was the wrong target. Call it a case of mistaken auto identity.

So that made Sonny a little less suspect in his girlfriend's murder, but not a whole lot less suspect overall.

Maybe he didn't kill Sharon Coleman, but maybe someone he pissed off was shooting at him and hit her instead. That seemed plausible given his astounding gift for making enemies of well-armed locals.

We also had to consider that Sharon Coleman was simply the victim of random gunfire and that no one benefited from killing her. In that case, our list of suspects was unlimited.

I told my guys that we couldn't rule out anyone in that apartment complex, which was infested with violent idiots.

We decided to let Sonny simmer for a bit. We looked at other reasons why someone would rake the complex with bullets that night.

HITTING RESET

Homicide investigations are often frustrating because all too often, your initial suspects may not pan out. Then you have to start over. This case made me crazy. Our initial focus was Sonny. We thought he might have been the intended target of the shooter, who sprayed the entire complex in the process.

We spent a lot of time tracking down all Sonny's enemies, but all too often, they had alibis or seemed to lack true bloodlust. One of these was his firecracker foe, the interesting young woman named China Doll. We tracked her down and brought her in for a talk.

I have to say, she initially made quite an impression. China Doll was of mixed race—African American and Asian—and absolutely stunning. Nineteen years old. Raven black hair and emerald eyes.

I thought, *Good Lord, who is this?*

But then she opened her mouth, and all the power of her physical beauty vanished as she unleashed a shrieking, vile stream of abuse that made the paint on the walls curdle.

I've been around the worst street creatures imaginable, and she made me want to grab my wife and children and move to a Tibetan monastery.

China Doll was a worst-case scenario waiting to happen. She was a known drug dealer with an outstanding warrant. When I reminded her of that, she shot daggers at me. Then I asked if she might have been involved in the murder of Sharon Coleman.

China Doll was not amused, but she was not stupid. She settled down and played nice—after I threatened to bust her on the warrant and throw her ass back in juvenile prison.

When I asked about her fireworks flare-up with Sonny, she played it down, saying he apologized a few days later and it was forgotten.

"We were cool," she said.

I had no real leverage over her, and her story had the ring of truth despite her obvious malice. I let her go, but later in the investigation, she would give up some key information.

Next up on our list of suspects was Peaches, whom Sonny had identified as his "other girlfriend," the one who had claimed to be carrying his child and threatened him with both a chair leg and a handgun if he kept seeing Sharon.

She had also made threats to kill Sharon. Peaches was definitely a gang groupie, so maybe she had one of them do her dirty work. We called her mother and had them pay us a visit at the station.

Peaches and China Doll must have read the same playbook. She came in playing the hard-ass, too. She was still a teenager and thus safe from being locked up in jail.

I put the fear of God into her, reminding her that being an accomplice to murder qualified her to be charged as an adult.

"We could throw you in with the big mean girls, Peaches. They'll have fun with you."

She mellowed but maintained that she had no reason to want Sharon dead. "I'm not pregnant," she said. "I never was. I was just trying to get Sonny back."

She also said she was in the apartment complex, getting her hair done by a friend, when the shooting occurred and Coleman was killed. She and her friends left, figuring rightly that police would soon descend. She had witnesses to back up her story. So we let her go with a promise to stay in touch.

TARGET OR COLLATERAL DAMAGE?

I called in all our homicide detectives and we regrouped. When we hit a dead end like that, I generally like to go back and review the crime scene evidence to see if anything fresh jumps out at me. In this case, I went down to the garage where the police lab keeps vehicles we've seized. I wanted to take another look at Sonny's car.

Our crime scene guys had been all through it and I'd read their reports, so I didn't expect to find anything new. I just wanted to go back over the evidence. I checked out the two bullet holes in the passenger-side door, and it struck me again, harder this time, that maybe this car wasn't the target.

Maybe it was just passing through the field of fire. Maybe the shooting had nothing to do with Sharon Coleman or Sonny or any of their enemies. Maybe they were just in the wrong place at the wrong time.

But if so, who or what was the real target for this crazed shooter?

Someone in that apartment complex knew the answer to that. Probably more than one. It was time to turn up the heat on the bad guys and girls, and the best way to do that is to bring them in on criminal charges and threaten them with prison time if they don't give us the straight story.

Given all the well-documented drug activity by gangbangers and their groupies in the apartment complex, I asked our Metro Vice Narcotics, and Intelligence Division to set up surveillance. I wanted to shake up the drug dealers and their customers and see what fell out of their pockets or their mouths.

My philosophy was always that our gang was tougher than their gang, and we had more toys. Narcotics cops are especially good at surveillance. They used a variety of vehicles and methods to get photographs and videos of the drug traffic in the complex.

All very low-key and stealthy. Even back then, before drones, we were way beyond the unmarked van sitting out front. The bad guys had no idea we were recording their every move. Our ninja narcs gathered up ample evidence of ongoing criminal activity so we could get search warrants for a raid.

BRINGING THE HEAT

Call me a Colorado cowboy, but I love a good roundup. We rode into the vipers' nest with a heavy show of force and a lot of noise, blowing doors off hinges and blinding 'em with stun grenades, known as "flashbangs."

We then filled up a couple of paddy wagons with the dazed and confused. We also collected massive amounts of evidence including rifles, shotguns, handguns, ammo, drugs, and some very incriminating photographs.

There was a method to our madness. The criminal activity we recorded gave us leverage to pry information out of those we hauled into the station. They were all tough and put up a united front until they were looking at serious time behind bars.

One of these was a seventeen-year-old, Amber, who was arrested in possession of illicit drugs that qualified her for a stretch in the big-person prison. She became much more cooperative when we laid out that unpleasant future.

Amber lived in the apartment complex. She and friends were "chillin'" there when the shooting started on the night of Sharon Coleman's death. They ran down the street to the home of a high school friend, Mike Wood, who lived with his parents.

They were hanging out in the basement so they wouldn't wake up his mother and brother. After a while, one of Mike's gangbanger buddies from Los Angeles showed up, and the party suddenly got very quiet.

According to Amber, the menacing stranger told her and her friends that he was sorry he'd scared them when he shot up their apartment complex.

"I wasn't shooting at you," he said. "I got a little trigger-happy with some East Coast Crips."

This was very welcome news.

"What was this guy's name?" we asked Amber.

This dude's name is "Khaki," she said.

A KHAKI KILLER?

According to Wood and others we interviewed, Khaki claimed to be a member of the Eighty-First Street Crips, and they were at war in our fair city with the local branch of the East Coast Crips, who had just moved into Amber's apartment building. The local yokels had established their own freelance drug dealership in competition with Khaki's Crips, who preferred to have a monopoly.

We learned from residents and informants that Khaki's shooting spree was meant to send the rival drug dealers a message that he was not a free-market advocate and that they had better shut down or be shut down.

He confessed all this to the girls on the night of the shooting but told them not to talk about it among themselves and their friends.

"This is some stuff we've got to keep between us," he warned them. "You know what I'm saying? We've got to keep this on the low level."

Khaki went on to make his point with a bit more emphasis, Amber told us. "He said if we say anything, he'll kill us all. I believed him. He is one scary dude."

Amber's assessment was on the money. I'm the first to question the authenticity of our local gang member wannabes, but when I checked with our gang unit, they said Khaki had bona fide credentials.

There is no Eighty-First Street in Colorado Springs, but there is in LA. Our man Khaki was a top lieutenant with an infamous affiliate of that city's South Central Crips, a well-organized national criminal enterprise that had established a presence in our town as part of its drug network expansion.

He was a true badass working on assignment from his LA gang leaders. He traveled back and forth between Los Angeles and Colorado Springs on red-eye flights, slipping in and out of town without drawing attention from authorities.

This was in the days before heavy security screenings of air passengers, so Khaki could go through airports carrying weapons and sacks full of his gang's drug profits. You might say Khaki was their Rocky Mountain regional sales representative—and hitman. LA gang experts said he was widely feared and known to be armed and dangerous.

Amber told us that she thought Khaki left our town and returned to LA after unleashing his deadly barrage of bullets on the apartment complex. Our roundup paid off. We walked away with a new likely suspect in the killing of Sharon Coleman.

WHAT'S IN A NICKNAME?

We had this dude's street name only, a physical description, and a reputation to track, but that was a good start. Nobody knows anyone's real name in the world of drugs and street gangs. They like it that way because it's harder to track them down.

But my gang of good guys had access to a national database of criminals and their aliases. It is called the Moniker File, or the AKA (Also Known As) File, and it often comes in very handy when tracking down nameless yahoos involved in crimes. The database also attached the real names, photos, and fingerprints to aliases and fake identities.

Like many gangbangers, Khaki had a long list of street names, although many of them were just mangled versions of "Khaki," which seemed to present spelling challenges for both law enforcement personnel and informants alike. My personal favorite version, found on some of our police reports, was "Kkkyha," which had a sort of ironic twist to it.

Khakee, Krakee, Kwaki—whatever! The shifty son of a bitch had a lengthy criminal record but had somehow avoided extended prison time. This investigation had already dragged on for three months, so I was determined to change that as quickly as possible.

Our chances of identifying someone were even better if the target of our desire had an unusual street name like Khaki. In his case, when we searched the Moniker File, we got a hit that identified him as Anthony Charles Blevells.

We put in a call to the LAPD and asked for any information their gangbusters and narcotics units had on him. They knew him well, by several names and nicknames. And as luck would have it, they had one of our target's known associates in custody, facing prison time and perhaps willing to play *Let's Make a Deal*, with Khaki as our prize behind curtain number one.

GOING HOLLYWOOD

I sent one of my ace detectives to LA that night on a red-eye flight, which sounds very Raymond Chandler, detective noirish. He wasn't there to look up anyone's Hollywood star. He had a date with a really bad actor, instead.

Let's call our informant "Homey," because he grew up in the same LA neighborhood as Khaki, and they had hung out there and in Colorado Springs over the years. Homey said Khaki had called him a week after the Coleman killing in my town and said he was coming back to LA.

"He told me, 'Oh, man! I was shooting at some East Coast Crips, and I smoked a bitch.'"

Our detective gritted his teeth and made a note of Khaki's cold, cold heart.

Homey added that Khaki had a fondness for AK-47s—the weapon used to kill Coleman and strike terror into the hearts of the entire apartment complex.

"He kept saying that the cops had nothing on him because he got rid of the gun by having someone throw it in the river," said our new best friend. "I'm not positive, but I think he said it was a river in Grand Junction."

Homey had been locked up for a while, and he claimed not to know Khaki's whereabouts. He also warned that along with multiple nicknames, his buddy from the hood had a suitcase full of fake IDs.

Our detective made a comment that we had identified his real name as Anthony Blevells, which brought a smile from Homey. He then coughed up a critical bit of information.

"Naw, man," Homey said. "That's what I thought, too. A lot of people say that's his real name, but it's not. That's just another of his fake names. I know his real name because one time I was at his mother's house with him and she called him 'Jude.'

"I asked about that later, and he said his real name was Jude Hood," Homey said. "I swear. You're never gonna find him, man. He's got a buncha fake IDs and he's got connections all over the country."

To which our guy replied: "Yeah, well, thanks for your concern, but my mother thinks I'm pretty smart, and I've got a few connections myself. See ya in the movies, man."

HEY, JUDE

Jude Hood? Now, THAT sounds like a fake name. In fact, we had a couple of other people mention that as one of the aliases he used, but we had believed that Anthony Charles Blevells was his real name.

You live and you learn. We checked it out, and sure enough, California had three records of him being arrested under that name for controlled substances, forgery, and vandalism, among other things. Even better, California records had a photo of him, and fingerprints. His real age was twenty-four.

We plugged all we had on Khaki and his multiple identities into yet another major resource, the National Crime Information Center. It's a vast database run by the FBI, and it provides the good guys who chase bad guys with an instantaneous connection to more than ninety thousand other local, state, and federal criminal justice and law enforcement agencies.

Within seconds of entering his information into the NCIC computer system, every lawman in the United States and Canada had access to that information and the fact that he was wanted in a murder case.

GRAND JURY TIME

By this time, we had put together a grand jury investigation to put pressure on all Khaki's playmates. Most law-abiding citizens may have heard of a grand jury investigation, but unless they've been called to serve on one or testify before one, they have little idea of what this critical tool can do to help detectives involved in a protracted and complex investigation.

To put it simply, the grand jury is a hammer and a vise for law enforcement. We often serve grand jury subpoenas to witnesses and suspects during protracted and complex investigations like the Sharon Coleman case. The goal is to force people to testify under oath. They are told that if they lie to a grand jury, we can charge them with first-degree perjury.

In a case like this, everyone lies. When dealing with a community of dope dealers and gun runners, you are shocked if someone actually tells the truth. To sort out the liars, the district attorney orders up a grand jury investigation, which has very wide subpoena power. Criminals and their defense lawyers hate grand juries, which is a good sign as far as I'm concerned.

Regular citizens are chosen from the voter rolls to serve on a grand jury. While they are usually timid at first, they soon learn that on a grand jury, they can ask questions of the witnesses, too. It doesn't take long before jurors are acting like hard-nosed cops and prosecutors themselves, taking notes on testimony, asking tough questions, and demanding answers. Their names are protected, so that makes them even more aggressive.

Grand jury cases are usually more interesting than run-of-the-mill criminal trials, and the jurors tend to bond with each other, the prosecutors, cops, and all the courthouse crowd. We had one lady who everyone hated to see go off grand jury duty, because she baked the best cookies in the world and brought them in every day. I wanted to have her called back, but you can serve only a year.

There is a strong element of drama and intensity in grand jury hearings, which, unlike regular trials, are conducted in secret. No press. No observers. Witnesses can bring their defense attorneys, but the lawyers are not allowed to ask questions or otherwise get involved. And if someone decides to "take the Fifth" so they don't incriminate themselves, we can lock their asses up without bond until they get tired of being in jail and decide to tell us what we want to know.

They lock the doors and put paper over the windows to the courtroom, so no one can hear or see what's going on inside during the grand jury hearings. Witnesses sit in the hallway, sweating out their turn. We like them a little rattled and scared, not knowing what is going on.

We don't let them talk to each other, because we don't want them conspiring to tell the same story. So they worry about getting caught in lies. As a result, it's not unusual for witnesses to go at each other in the hallway.

They also can say crazy things on the stand because they get confused and think this isn't a real trial. I love it when that happens.

We once had a guy who was under investigation for robbery, kidnapping, and homicide. He was dumb as a rock, and dangerous. We had belly chains on him. When the DA said, "What is your occupation?" he just stared at him.

I was sitting next to the DA, and I tugged on his jacket and said, "He doesn't know what 'occupation' means."

"What do you do to earn a living?" the DA said.

"I rob people," said our guy.

The grand jury gasped. His defense lawyer put his hands over his face.

Trying to recover, the bad guy then let rip with this statement: "But I ain't never killed no motherfucker!"

Just for kicks, I then suggested that the DA ask this doofus what he does every morning.

His response to that question was the same thing he had once told me: "I go to my friend Stanley's crib, and we look for places to rob."

After that testimony, I thought the grand jury was just going to bring out a rope and hang him on the spot.

But again, I digress. Back to the vipers' nest!

CAUGHT IN A LIE

With the grand jury underway, our investigation homed in on Khaki, the man of a hundred identities. He did have a lot of friends—or, at least, a lot of people who were afraid of being his enemy. They were prepared to lie for him, even under oath, so we asked each one of them if protecting Khaki was worth ten years in prison for perjury.

"We will charge you with that, convict you, and put you away for that amount of time if you don't tell us the truth," we said.

We weren't playing nice. When you are dealing with criminals and lowlifes, the old saw about catching more flies with honey does not apply. Only the hammer and the vise and threats of long-term incarceration work with the hard-core crew.

"We will destroy your life and lock you up with people who will break you and use you every day for their own purpose and pleasure." This is strong motivation, in my experience.

Loyalty and even fear of revenge go out the window when you paint that picture. And then I always add, "I never make a promise I can't keep, and I never make a threat I can't carry out, so when I tell you that I'm going to fuck up your life, you can believe I will do it until you tell me the truth."

Those were my parting words before we brought them before the grand jury. In this case, the hearing ran about a month and a half. We caught lies right and left. We charged five people with perjury and told them they wouldn't see their families for ten years if they didn't cooperate with our investigation.

The teenager Mike Wood, who befriended Khaki, was one of those charged with perjury. Several of the ladies from the apartment complex had fled to his parents' house after the shooting.

In his grand jury testimony, Wood confirmed that Khaki had claimed to be the shooter, but we caught him in a couple of other lies. He initially claimed that he hadn't seen Khaki since the night of the shooting, but we'd heard a different story from others, so we charged him with perjury.

That hammer and vise would prove very helpful a few months later.

At that point, we had Khaki identified by his real name and aliases. We had his fingerprints. We also had an October 16, 1991, grand jury indictment charging Jude Hood (and all his aliases) with murder. The charge was based on an element in the statute saying that if a person engages in conduct that "manifests an extreme indifference to the value of human life," and a death results, that person will be charged with murder in the first degree.

The spraying of bullets into an occupied building and a parking lot full of cars certainly qualifies.

We had Khaki and all his names listed with law enforcement agencies across the country and beyond, knowing that he was a very smart operator with a history of eluding arrest. But then, eighteen days after the murder indictments came down, Khaki made a mistake.

Or maybe he'd prefer to blame it on Kevin Dandre Freeman.

On November 4, Louisiana State Police contacted us and said they had arrested a Colorado man of that name with two other individuals, in a traffic stop near Lake Charles. They had locked them up after finding three pounds of cocaine and about four ounces of marijuana in the vehicle, along with several guns.

They called us because that vehicle, a 1990 Chevy with Colorado plates, was registered to our ghostly friend Anthony C. Blevells, who was not in the vehicle when it was pulled over, according to all the driver's licenses confiscated by the Louisiana troopers.

Very interesting. We had our guys check the Colorado Department of Motor Vehicles to see if they had a driver's license photo of Kevin Dandre Freeman. They did.

"Kevin" had obtained that license just one month and a day after Sharon Coleman's murder. And, lo and behold, when we compared it to the photograph we had of Khaki, a.k.a. Jude Hood, a.k.a. Anthony C. Blevells, well, you can probably guess that they were either identical twins or one and the same person.

We confirmed that they were the same guy, by comparing fingerprints from "Kevin" taken in Louisiana to those of "Anthony" on file in our own records. We then asked our partners in crime-stopping in Louisiana to please ship Jude Hood and all his aliases back to Colorado Springs. They agreed to do so, no doubt glad to be rid of him.

Once we had him back in our loving arms, we sat down with ol' Khaki. I try to be congenial in these chats, so I started by introducing myself, but I barely got out my rank before Khaki suggested I shove something unpleasant where the sun doesn't shine.

He then refused to answer any questions and demanded that his lawyer be summoned. I tried to charm him, but he seemed oblivious to my charms. He lawyered up and shut up.

Our strongest evidence against him was the statement he allegedly made to our informant in LA about the shooting. A good defense attorney can make hash of statements by someone trying to trade information to lighten his own sentence.

Juries tend to be skeptical about informants like that, as well.

SEARCHING FOR THE WEAPON

We needed physical evidence linking Khaki to the shooting. I had our guys go back to Khaki's conversation with Mike Wood and the ladies at his parents' house on the night of the murder.

We have always wondered why someone as careful and crafty as Khaki even bothered to show up at the home of a sixteen-year-old kid whose gang connections were not all that strong.

During the grand jury hearings, we caught Wood in a couple of lies, so we charged him with perjury. We called his parents and had them bring him in, hoping we could get more out of him under threat of a prison term.

The teenager admitted that he'd been scared to tell us the entire story. Khaki had actually called him two days after the shooting and asked him for "a favor" in exchange for a small amount of dope.

"What's the favor?" Wood asked.

Khaki then asked Wood to dump several parts of a disassembled AK-47 that he would give him. At the time, Wood didn't know that it was the same type of weapon used in the fatal shooting of Sharon Coleman.

At first, Wood wasn't sure how to get rid of the parts, which included the rifle barrel with the serial number on it. Khaki told him to try to file down the serial number, but he couldn't manage that.

As it turned out, Wood's parents, who had been trying to steer him out of the gang's reach, asked him to go fishing with his younger brother the following weekend. He had always refused, but after getting the gun parts from Khaki, he went along with them to the Rampart Range Reservoir, a beautiful spot up in Pike National Forest, about twenty-five miles northwest of Colorado Springs.

He put the gun parts in his fishing-pole case. It was pretty sad. The kid's father felt bad that they were always butting heads over the gang. He thought maybe the son had finally come around when he went fishing with the family that day.

But Wood went only so he could toss Khaki's gun parts into the lake while pretending to toss stones into the water. His parents thought it was a glorious day of fishing until we showed up at the front door and said, "Your son is under arrest for being an accessory to first-degree murder."

A few days later, we took Wood and his parents to the reservoir, which is a main water source for the city of Colorado Springs, and a favorite place for hiking, canoeing, and fishing. We had our doubts that we would find what we were looking for.

The lake is thirteen miles around and a hundred feet deep in some areas. Unlike on the teen's visit months earlier, there was snow on the ground. We feared he would have no idea where he had tossed the parts.

Wood, who was all about cooperation by then, surprised us. He had no trouble identifying at least three spots where he'd thrown the gun parts. We were primarily interested in the rifle barrel with the serial numbers on it. The teen said he remembered throwing it in the water near a large rock, which he easily located that day.

"It's in that little inlet area," he said, pointing to a shallow spot near the shore.

There was a hole in the ice in that particular area. The next day, our team of divers went down. It took them only twenty minutes to find the barrel of an AK-47. It was cold, but it was worth it.

We finally had the physical evidence we needed to convict Khaki: a murder weapon, or at least a big part of it. This was evidence that would be hard for a defense attorney to dispute.

Not that they didn't try, of course.

The legal wrangling and deal making went on for a couple of years, but in the end, Khaki gave up and pleaded guilty to second-degree murder in February 1993, in the July 1991 killing of Sharon Coleman.

He was sentenced to twenty years in prison.

It was one of the tougher cases we had in a very tough year or two or three. I wish I could say it was satisfying for everyone to see Khaki locked up, but the victim's family was very bitter, and I can't say that I blame them.

As they said at the sentencing hearing, her life was priceless to them, and she was killed for no reason at all, other than being in the wrong place at the wrong time when a violent scumbag decided to light up an entire complex with a deadly weapon.

Evil prevailed.

We secured some justice, but I fully understood the Coleman family's anger when one of them told the media that she would have preferred to see Khaki shot in the stomach and chest and left to bleed out.

CHAPTER EIGHT:
TWISTED SISTERS

THE TRIGGER: JEALOUSY, REVENGE, AND RAGE

If you become a murder victim—and I certainly hope that never happens (for your sake, not mine)—odds are that your killer will be someone you know, especially if you are a woman.

We've all heard that absence makes the heart grow fonder. Does that mean that closeness makes the heart grow colder?

The FBI reports that in 2017, 28 percent of homicide victims were killed by someone they knew other than family members. Another 12.3 percent were slain by family members, and 9.7 percent were killed by strangers. In the other 50 percent of cases, the killer's relationship to the victim was not known.

If that doesn't make you become a recluse, how about this? A 2018 Global Report from the United Nations found that of the 87,000 females who were murdered around the world in the previous year, the majority were killed by their "intimate partners" or family members.

The report noted that about 137 women are killed by a loved one every single day. And a stunning 58 percent of all female homicide victims were killed by their nearest and dearest.

You won't see *that* on a Valentine's Day card anytime soon.

So there is a very good reason why those of us in the homicide-detective trade always look carefully at spouses and lovers, especially when working a case with a female victim like the late Mona King, featured in this case.

HOME SWEET HOME, UNSWEETENED

Raymond Lee King was a hardworking electrician who advanced to the position of supervisor in his company because his bosses really liked him. At the age of thirty-five, he was on a good track with a solid job, earning a comfortable salary, with big plans for his later years.

Things were going well at home, too. Ray had an attractive, churchgoing wife. Mona, thirty-six, was a former high school homecoming queen who worked in a savings and loan and was known for being prim and proper.

In fact, she belonged to a very conservative fundamentalist Christian group called the Way International, which claimed forty thousand members worldwide. A fiery bunch, they supposedly spoke in tongues and trained with firearms. (I'm not all that religious, but I've been known to do both myself, though rarely at the same time.)

Married six years, Ray and Mona had a five-year-old daughter, Tara, who could have been on the cover of *Toddler Life Magazine* if there were such a thing. She was a beautiful child with golden hair like lemon meringue.

This future homecoming queen was always dressed like a princess, with frilly dresses and patent leather shoes. Those shiny little-girl shoes were harder than a steel-toed work boot, by the way. I say that from painful experience.

By late 1984, life was pretty darn good for the King family, and they probably would have lived happily ever after if not for the less-happy marriage of someone else in Mona's family.

Mona's older sister, Carla Cannon, thirty-eight, had married a chiropractor and lived about 280 miles west of Colorado Springs, in the Western Slope hiking, biking, and wine-drinking town of Grand Junction, Colorado.

Then, suddenly, Carla didn't live there anymore.

She showed up at the front door of Ray and Mona's happy home in an unhappy state. With luggage. A lot of luggage. Most of it packed with shoes. Carla had more high heels than the Rockettes. She was all about the kicks, too.

Carla was a piece of work. She had left her husband and Grand Junction after some not-so-grand dysfunction.

Let's call it a "social disconnect."

She was social. He wasn't.

She was a party girl. He was a chiropractor.

They rubbed each other the wrong way. Theirs was the age-old story of marriages torn asunder.

Some people change. Others don't. So they change partners.

Carla wanted more fun out of life. Don might have wanted the same. But hanging out in bars, drinking, dancing, and flirting with strangers wasn't his idea of fun.

So they split. Their two teenagers opted to stay home with Don after the divorce.

Maybe Carla just wasn't into motherhood. Maybe she still felt like a teenager herself. She certainly acted like one.

SWINGING IN THE SPRINGS

After moving into the Kings' house in Colorado Springs, Carla hit the swinging-singles bars all over town. She was not subtle. Carla was a looker who dressed to display her assets. She was a magnet for men on the make. She loved 'em and left 'em.

Lounge lizards were soon circling and panting in packs. Still, she didn't like trolling the meat markets on her own. She needed a wing woman, or at least a designated driver, and Mona was Carla's first choice for a running mate.

Churchgoing Mona begged off at first. She had grown content playing it straight as a working wife and mother. But her older sister badgered her. She worked on Mona, saying her life was boring and that she needed to get out and enjoy herself more.

Unfortunately for his marriage, Mona's husband, Ray, was too busy working to counter Carla's relentless recruitment of his Bible-loving, straitlaced wife.

Relentless, Carla managed to plant a bug in Mona's ear, or somewhere. She would share her party-girl stories with Mona while Ray was working, telling her about all the good-lookin' good ol' boys lined up to buy her drinks and dance her pants off in the local dens of sin.

She poured it on, trying to loosen up her little sis with a double shot of FOMO.

"You're missing out on all the fun," she teased. "Life is too short."

She worked on Mona as if she were dry-sanding driftwood, wearing her down by making her feel like a boring old housewife with dishpan hands.

Our siblings, like our parents, know how to push our buttons because, in many cases, they installed those buttons as we were growing up.

After a few weeks of sis-dissing, Mona decided that Carla had a point. Ray worked all the time. She was often left at home all night with Tara while he went out on emergency calls for customers.

Then he would come home exhausted and fall asleep, snoring like a banshee.

Her church, the Way, wasn't a lot of laughs, either. She and other women members complained that the men in charge felt it was their Way or the highway. Being a good and godly girl was hard enough without being bullied by righteous gasbags.

TIME OUT

Now, as you might imagine, Carla's campaign to lure his wife from him and their golden child and into the taverns and dance halls, did not sit well with Raymond Lee King. But he had little power to stop the sisters from traipsing out to trip the light fantastic when he was called out for work at all hours.

Ray felt helpless as he watched conniving Carla set the bait and lure Mona into her tawdry world. Before he knew it, his wife began coming home reeking of booze, cigarette smoke, and other men's cologne.

He blamed Carla for the growing divide between them. Mona blamed Raymond for caring only about his job and neglecting her.

Tensions rose. Tempers flared.

Ray's hurt and confusion gave way to a simmering rage. Every dinner conversation blew up into a confrontation. Divorce was thrown onto the table.

His life, their life, and their child's life had turned toxic because of the evil sister's manipulations and Mona's lack of a moral spine, or so Raymond concluded.

The warring couple held it together through the holidays, but by March 1985, Raymond couldn't stand to be in the same house with the twisted sisters. He loaded up his truck and moved out.

He took shelter forty-five miles south in a Pueblo, Colorado, McMansion where his younger brother was house-sitting for a wealthy friend of the family.

Your friendly homicide detective narrator would like to step in here and offer a helpful bit of unsolicited advice. I am not a board-certified psychiatrist or even a shade-tree shrink, but in a long career of finding one spouse aerated by lead and the other holding a smoking gun, I have learned a thing or two.

If your marriage goes to shit, sure, take a time-out and give each other some space if you think it's a good idea—or just necessary for your survival. But for the love of Zeus, do not take shelter in a home with wall-to-wall weaponry owned by an avid gun collector.

Which is what Raymond Lee King did.

Estrangement did not make his heart grow fonder. But it did give Raymond some free time to hone his sharpshooting skills with a variety of collectible firearms. Reading marital guidance books or even collecting beer cans might have been a wiser way to spend his idle hours.

A pissed-off husband with easy access to an arsenal? Well, that can lead to all sorts of sad scenarios, and often does.

NEURAL HIJACKING

Not to sound like an old Porter Wagoner country tune, but Raymond couldn't live with his wife, and he couldn't live without her.

The thought of losing his wife and his daughter and all his dreams for their future together scrambled his brain. He was a certified electrician. He could fix blown circuits in an office tower or apartment complex, but he didn't have the tools to handle his own emotional overload.

Desperate for help, he decided to go to the source of his sister-sibling torment: Kansas City. Home of his in-laws, the parents of Mona and Carla.

I know, asking your in-laws for help when your marriage is falling apart seems like a crazed man's worst move to me, too, but maybe Raymond thought the parents shared his concerns about their girls forming a honky-tonk tag team.

Maybe he thought they'd help him figure out how to win back his wife.

Hard to say what he was thinking, but Ray took a rare week off from work and hit the road for KC on a weekend when he had little Tara with him.

We don't know what transpired with the in-laws. We don't know what was said or whose side they took or didn't take. We do know that the trip to Kansas City did nothing to relieve Raymond's distress.

We also know that he repeatedly told his in-laws that he did not want a divorce. But his position on that changed when little Tara let slip that Mona was spending nights at the home of another man.

A few days later, Raymond consulted with an attorney about obtaining a divorce and securing custody of Tara. His decision to throw in the towel may have been logical given his wife's infidelity, but it did not bring closure for Ray, whose rage and despair made for a deadly mix.

SISTER-CIDE

Raymond King had another court-ordered visitation with his daughter on the weekend of March 23–24, 1985. After picking her up, however, he dropped the child off with his father, Cecil King.

"I need to talk to Mona about the divorce," he told his dad.

Ray did not return on Sunday to pick up his daughter. He didn't show up on Monday, either.

Cecil King tried calling both Ray and Mona. Neither responded.

He found a babysitter for Tara and went looking for Ray. His first stop was the Colorado Springs home where Mona had remained after the breakup.

Cecil rang the doorbell. No answer. He peered in through the front windows of the house but couldn't see anything. He then walked around to the back of the house and looked into the windows there.

I wish I could tell you that he saw his son and Mona locked in a tearful and loving embrace as they pledged to renew their love and rebuild their marriage for the sake of their beautiful child.

Sorry. A homicide detective is not in the wish-fulfillment business, and this isn't a Hollywood rom-com with a happily-ever-after ending. You knew that when you opened this book. I spent a long career bearing—and baring—the bad news. This case was no different.

I got the call after Ray's father saw a body on the kitchen floor, surrounded by blood. Cecil King ran to a neighbor's house and called 911.

I was at the station, talking with my homicide team about another investigation, when the call came in. I grabbed a couple of my guys and we headed to the Kings' house.

Our patrolmen were already there, along with a pack of gawking neighbors. Our guys had forced entry into the locked house. Even before we arrived on the scene, the body count had doubled.

"Be advised, a second victim was found dead at the scene. Both with multiple gunshot wounds."

The female in the kitchen was blond, wearing a halter top and shorts. She had at least five gunshot wounds to the head and chest.

The second victim was in the living room. She had been shot at least seven times, front and back. Her car keys were on the floor, by her hand. A purse strap was slung on her arm, and a jacket lay next to her body.

She had walked into a barrage of bullets. Her killer had dropped her before she could turn and run.

Cecil King identified the victims as his daughter-in-law, Mona, found in the living room, and her sister, Carla Cannon, found in the kitchen. There was no forced entry into the house. No sign of anything taken.

With two victims dispatched, the shooter had fled.

You know I hate it when murderers have a head start. They dump weapons, destroy evidence, and head for the hills while my team and I are still assessing the situation.

I don't like playing catch-up, but I love a challenge. And this wasn't my first rodeo.

At that point, none of my team knew the sad saga of the wayward sisters, the distraught and angry husband, and the marriage in tatters. But the crime scene talked to me, and it spoke volumes.

Since there was no forced entry and nothing missing, this was not an armed robbery or a burglary interrupted. Our runner had come to kill. The sheer number of shots taken screamed that these murders were personal. The triggers for these killings were clearly vengeance, jealousy, and rage.

The final shot to Mona's head was a mob-style close-range bullet to the temple, a professional assassin's coup de grâce death blow.

No guns were found at the scene, which did not bode well for anyone in the killer's path of flight. We had to find this shooter before someone else went down.

The crime scene also presented us with a bloody shoe print of a pointed toe—most likely a cowboy boot. Even more interesting were the scattered bullet casings—twelve of them, likely from two pistols unless the killer paused to reload.

Our crime scene crew said the casings were from an older-model .22 revolver, one that had not been made since the 1960s. I found that information quite helpful.

TOOLS OF DESTRUCTION

I am always grateful when a killer chooses a distinctive weapon instead of a run-of-the-mill Saturday night special or a steak knife from a kitchen drawer.

A unique weapon can help us narrow the field of suspects considerably. My favorite example of this occurred in my early days as a homicide detective. I had a case in which the male victim had been fatally beaten. His head was bashed in during a robbery in the parking lot of a Target store.

This poor guy was just a truck driver delivering Christmas ornaments to Target. He had an eighteen-wheeler full of holiday baubles. His only crime was tardiness.

He arrived after this particular Target had closed, so he did what tardy truckers do. He pulled into the parking lot, shut down the engine, and went to sleep in his little trucker nest behind the driver's seat.

While the trucker slumbered all snug in his bed, some asshole broke in and bashed his head. (My apologies if I just desecrated your favorite Christmas poem.)

We figured the motive was robbery since the back door of the trailer had been forced open. The driver probably heard all the clatter and sprang from his cab to see what was the matter. (I'm on a roll.)

The crime scene didn't give us much. An inventory of the truck turned up only about thirty-five dollars in missing Christmas ornaments. The autopsy gave us only a little more to work with.

The coroner shaved the victim's head to get a better look at his wounds, which were unusual. The murder weapon appeared to be made of heavy metal and precisely engineered. There were deep gouges in his skull, each of them exactly ten millimeters apart.

Obviously, this wasn't the usual baseball bat, crowbar, or billy club. The coroner speculated that maybe it was a forged tool of some kind.

My mind can be a vast and empty place at times, but every now and then a spark flares up. When the coroner said "forged tool," just that sort of flash occurred. There was a Forge Road in an industrial area of Colorado Springs.

One of the companies on that road, not coincidentally, was Western Forge, which, at the time, made the Craftsman-brand tools for Sears Roebuck. It was kind of a local-pride thing that such a well-regarded American brand of tools was made in our town.

Fun fact with a twist: Western Forge has been known as the largest American manufacturer of screwdrivers. Impressive, right?

I figured the hometown company must have some pretty sharp engineers on staff, and maybe they could help identify the murder weapon used on our poor trucker's head. It was worth a shot.

So I drove to their no-frills stucco-and-glass headquarters at the edge of the Rockies, introduced myself to the honchos, and told them about the case of the trucker beaten to death for a handful of Christmas ornaments.

"If I gave you the dimensions of the gouges in his head, do you think you could tell me what sort of tool might have been used to kill him?" I asked.

The tool guys aren't often invited to help solve murder cases. They were all over it. Manufacturing engineers also love a challenge, especially one involving precise measurements. Bless their calculating little hearts.

They eagerly informed me that their international association of tool manufacturers keeps files on the dimensions of all tools to protect patents and licenses and all that stuff.

So we had a big database they could search.

Being engineers, they did not trust the measurements taken at the coroner's office. They wanted to see photos of the wounds.

"Are you sure?" I asked tactfully. "They are not pleasant to view."

"No problem, man. I can handle it," one of them said. "I was in the Army Reserve."

I whipped out a large full-color photo of the trucker's bashed head and put it on his drawing board.

Mr. Army Reserve went white and promptly lost his lunch in his wastebasket.

"Would you and your trash can of puke please leave the room before you make me and your entire team vomit?" I asked.

I'm always working for the greater good.

After reviewing the photos and taking measurements, the other engineers were looking a little pasty, too. They asked if I would give them a few days to do their own research and calculation.

"No problem, gents," I said.

By that time, I was ready for some fresh mountain air myself.

They spent three days playing tool detectives. Then they had me return for their findings. I entered the conference room, where they were set up for a very professional presentation.

The engineers laid out their findings as if they were pitching a new set of wrenches for Mr. Sears and Mr. Roebuck. I was impressed!

"We've decided these wounds could have been made by three possible items. Number one would be a main support leg for a surveyor's transit. (You've seen guys standing on the highway taking measurements with these telescope-looking things on a tripod.)

"Number two would be [some other weird type of machinery part that I can't remember], and number three would be a bumper jack out of a 1972 General Motors product."

Jackpot!

A bumper jack made perfect sense. The killer probably used it to pry open the back door of the truck trailer and then beat the trucker with the jack when confronted.

I congratulated the tool geeks on their detective work and may have promised them that they'd never have to pay a speeding ticket again. (Don't hold me to that one.)

I left tool town with my first decent clue in the case. Within a few weeks, we identified a suspect who drove a 1972 Cadillac. His nickname was Big Red, and he was known as a violent guy with larceny in his heart.

We arrested him and seized his Caddie's bumper jack. He had cleaned it with gasoline, very thoroughly. Lucky for us, he forgot that it was hollow inside. We found hairs that matched those of the bashed trucker, and took Big Red to jail on a murder charge.

And *that*, my friend, is my favorite example of a unique murder weapon leading us to the killer.

I hope you enjoyed this brief interlude. Now, back to our mystery of the twisted sisters and their tragic end.

THE USUAL SUSPECTS

The bullet casings found at the crime scene gave us a fix on the murder weapon or weapons. We knew they were fired from 1960s vintage revolvers, but we still had to find guns and a suspect we could link to them.

In the meantime, Cecil King filled us in on the family drama involving his son, his son's wife, and the older sister who stirred the pot. He told us about Carla's bad influence on Mona and about Ray's despair over his wayward wife and their impending divorce.

Ray was definitely our prime suspect, especially since he had disappeared shortly after his wife and sister-in-law were murdered in his former home.

I wondered if Ray might have gone off to commit suicide. While we looked for him, we also checked for other possible suspects lurking in the dive bars where the sisters had partied.

Everywhere we looked, lounge lizards slithered out from under rocks.

Carla and Mona were both well known in local honky-tonks, where they drank, danced, and dazzled male admirers. We took an interest in one particular Goodtime Charlie, a bar fixture who sported gold chains and a Members Only jacket.

He considered himself a smooth operator. I surmised that he probably drove a high-mileage muscle car with a red Naugahyde interior—made from the soft underbellies of baby Naugas.

We homed in on him because at first he had denied dating Mona, but then he admitted they had hooked up a time or two. Still, Charlie didn't seem capable of commitment, let alone murder. He didn't know much about Mona's life beyond the bar.

Goodtime Charlie wasn't into deep relationships. He was all touchy, no feely.

Since he had a decent alibi and didn't seem emotionally involved with Mona or anyone else, we put Charlie on the back burner.

Besides, Raymond Lee King was clearly our front-runner for double homicide, especially after we talked to his brother, Bob, at the Pueblo house where they'd been staying.

Bob told us that on the Saturday before the dead sisters were found, Ray borrowed his silver-and-blue Ford Ranger pickup truck. Neighbors told us that on the weekend of the murders, they had seen a vehicle of that description in the driveway of Ray's former home, where Mona and Carla lived.

Bob also connected us to the possible murder weapons.

"Ray sometimes borrows guns from the collection of the guy who owns this house," the brother said. "He did some target shooting out back."

We tracked down their absentee landlord, who said his collection included a pair of Smith & Wesson Model 17s—the .22-caliber six-shot revolvers that matched up with the twelve spent casings found at the murder scene.

The owner gave us permission to search his home and check out the collection. When we did an inventory with him, we found that those two revolvers were missing, along with fifty rounds of ammo, which meant Ray was likely still armed and dangerous.

When I asked his brother where Ray might have gone to hide out, he told us that our suspect owned a wooded seven-acre lot in a high-end residential development outside Colorado Springs. It seemed that Ray had planned on building a dream home there for his family, before that dream went sour.

I asked the sheriff's department to send a deputy to that location, just in case Ray was hiding out there. It also occurred to me that he might have gone there to take his own life after killing Mona and Carla.

The deputies didn't see any sign of Ray at his luxury lot, so the search continued. We put out a bulletin on the Ford Ranger borrowed from his brother. Every law enforcement officer in the region was on the lookout.

I figured that if Ray was still alive, we'd find him before long.

I figured right.

The next morning, the Colorado State Patrol notified us that they'd nabbed him after troopers spotted the pickup on Interstate Highway 25 and pulled it over between Pueblo and Colorado Springs.

Ray didn't put up a fight even though he had two loaded revolvers and thirty rounds in the truck and his pants pockets. We confiscated his clothing and cowboy boots. Dried blood found on those items matched that of his murdered wife and sister-in-law.

We found you, Ray!

But we still had to make sure he paid for his crimes.

RAY'S STORY

When I went out to interview Ray at one of our police substations, two defense attorneys were already trying to get to him. I had to explain to them—even though they already knew damned well—that while Ray had a right to an attorney, there is nothing that says every attorney has a right to a client.

In other words, I wasn't about to let them talk to Ray unless our suspect demanded to talk to them.

Call me selfish, but I preferred to talk to Ray before they did.

Ray agreed with that plan. Our talk was very informative, though not at all engaging. He appeared to be in a zombie state.

We'd heard that Ray was a mellow, even dull dude, but when I talked to him, he was close to catatonic. This was understandable. Killing your wife and her sister might tend to have a deleterious impact on your state of mind.

Ray had not killed himself, as I'd feared, but he had killed off any feelings or fears. His tank was empty. He had been a salt-of-the-earth kind of guy, who had never been violent in the past.

Then Carla came to town and recruited his wife as her wing woman. Ray lost his family, and then he lost control. Not that slaughtering two people is excusable under any circumstances. It's just that these weren't the sort of people you'd expect to be caught up in a violent crime. They were middle-class Americans living the dream until the trajectory of their lives changed dramatically.

For the worse.

When I interviewed Ray, I laid out our case: His brother's borrowed pickup in the driveway. Blood on his boots. The murder weapons in his possession. The shell casings. The all-too-obvious motive.

Ray gave me the dead-man stare and proceeded to confess, with a lame-assed twist from a dime-store novel. He claimed he took the guns only to force Mona to sit down and listen to him as he begged her to come back.

His supposed plan went awry when she wasn't home. He walked in and found Carla instead. So, he decided to wait for his wife.

Ray claimed that he had put the guns down but Carla grabbed one of them. He said he tried to take the pistol away from her, and during the struggle, she was shot.

"The damn thing went off," he said.

Yeah, Ray, the damned gun went off. *Five times*, Ray?

His explanation for the multiple gunshots was this: "She was sitting on the floor bleeding and she said, "Shoot me more so I don't suffer."

Sure, Ray, I find that shooting victims do tend to beg for more.

When did Mona enter the picture, Ray?

"Well, I was gonna shoot myself, and then Mona walked in the door . . . and I don't remember what happened after that."

How convenient.

I'd had enough. Ray had confessed to the murder of his sister-in-law. The courts would sort out the rest of the case as presented to them in our reports.

MAKING IT STICK

Murder cases can drag on for years, even after the killer has been caught. Everything homicide detectives do is under a microscope. You have to be extremely cautious you don't overlook things or take shortcuts during an investigation.

You get the search warrants and follow all the rules. Defense attorneys either try to prove that we are incompetent, which doesn't usually sit well with juries, or try to convince the jury that we are evil and do bad-cop things like planting evidence and framing suspects.

If neither of those tactics looks feasible, they'll go with, "My guy did it, but he didn't mean to. He was crazy, provoked, drunk, drugged, and incompetent to stand trial."

Murder trials are a sophisticated high-stakes game. That is why I never charged someone until I had proved everything beyond a reasonable doubt. I wanted my cases nailed down so tight, they couldn't be torn up with a jackhammer.

Defense attorneys draw a line down a yellow legal pad. On the left, they write down facts the jury will believe. On the right is a list of facts that the jury might doubt. If the list of facts in doubt exceeds the list of believable facts, the defense will take the case to trial. If the believable facts outnumber those in doubt, the defense will likely try to make a deal for their client.

The lawyer's game has nothing to do with true guilt or true innocence.

It's all about getting the client off by any means possible. My job was to keep that list of possibilities very short.

In Ray's case, we went to trial and the jury swiftly rendered a decision, finding him guilty on two counts of first-degree murder. He was sentenced to two consecutive life sentences.

I left the courtroom feeling that justice was served. My team and I had done our jobs and served the public interest. Even so, I took no joy in the destruction of this family and all its hopes and dreams. I felt sadness for them, especially the daughter who had lost both her mother and her father.

That sadness came over me when I saw little Tara with her grandparents outside the courtroom, after Ray was sentenced to prison for the rest of his life. My sadness deepened when she walked up to me and said sweetly, "Did you put my daddy in jail?"

I don't lie to children.

"Yes, I did."

Little Tara then reared back and delivered a swift kick to my shin.

And that is how I came to know just how hard the toe on a little girl's patent leather shoe can be.

CHAPTER NINE:
LOWLIFES DESERVE JUSTICE, TOO

THE TRIGGER: MONEY

On Sunday, November 9, 1986, my homicide team received a report that a maintenance guy at the Armadillo Motel in Colorado Springs had discovered a body after finding the door to a guest room cracked open.

When he looked inside, he saw a male on the floor who appeared to be "cold," as in dead cold.

"There is a lot of blood around him," the motel manager said.

Well, that doesn't sound good for him, now, does it?

I was heading out for a morning jog before work when our dispatcher called me. At the time, I was the detective sergeant in charge of homicide investigations for the Colorado Springs Police Department.

The dispatcher said the fire department rescue had responded already. They called it in as a DOA, possible homicide.

Highly possible, I thought.

I wasn't all that excited about jogging anyway.

I knew the Armadillo Motel. Crime checked in on a regular basis there. It was in the oldest part of town, the west side. The area had a certain rugged-trending-to-rancid 1950s charm. If you owned a house there, chances were that you'd been born in it and you would die in it.

The residential areas of the west side weren't particularly high in crime. A lot of low-functioning lowlifes were scattered around in rental properties and fly-by-night hotels. Most weren't violent. They were more likely to be prey than predator.

In this part of town, high school graduates were overachievers. The typical rap sheet in this neighborhood included auto theft, burglary, minor battery, driving while intoxicated, walking while intoxicated, being stupid while intoxicated, being drugged into stupefaction, and other numbskullduggery.

And yes, as you may have surmised, the Armadillo Motel was not the Ritz Carlton. It was more of a no-tell motel dump. Rumor had it that to get a reservation for the Armadillo, you needed to show proof of a criminal record.

(I'm told that recently the hotel in that location used a monster bedbug as its Facebook page profile photo.)

When I went to room 22 there back in 1986, the crime scene featured a dead Black male in blood-soaked clothing, as advertised. He was upright, with his back against the ratty couch, sitting in a pool of blood.

He had multiple stab wounds in his face, neck, chest, back, and arm. The final tally by the coroner would be in the neighborhood of more than twenty-seven stab wounds.

This was not a stranger-on-stranger murder. This was personal. Whoever killed this victim was very angry with him about something.

The victim's wallet was in his hip pocket. A Colorado identification card said he was Eric Stanley Houston, born October 1, 1954.

One look around the room said he was a bottom feeder in the pool of life, just a paycheck away from sleeping under an overpass.

I took a tour of the crime scene, which was brief given that this was a motel room impersonating an apartment. The room looked as though it had been decorated with a live grenade. Hard to tell what had been disturbed in the life-and-death battle versus what was just part of the preexisting squalor.

We could rule out death by tidiness. Clothing, socks, and shoes were scattered everywhere. It looked as if a Goodwill drop box had been dumped in the room or else exploded.

Usually, when you find a broken glass pane on the front door of a murder scene, you can assume it was broken during the commission of the crime. Not here. Glass from the door pane was found scattered outside the door and on the floor just inside the hotel room. It looked as if it had been there a long time, so maybe breaking and entering wasn't how the killer got in.

A couple of wayward stereo speaker cables were lying about—one on the sidewalk outside the door, and the other on a table inside—raising the prospect of a burglary along with the murder.

There were blood spatters on the concrete walkway outside the apartment and on the threshold, indicating that maybe the killer was bleeding, too. There were also round blood droplets scattered all over the room. These indicated that maybe whoever stabbed Mr. Houston was also cut in the process.

Not to give away too much from my personal CSI toolkit, but injuries to the hand of the attacker are quite common when there is a lot of blood being sprayed during a multiple stabbing. The blood lubricates the knife handle, and often the stabber's hand will slide down onto the blade and cause a gash while the attacker is wielding the knife with great force.

The round droplets scattered all over were typical of gravity bleeding, or blood dripping from a wound. We found blood all over the bed, in the bathroom, and in the kitchen sink. There was a long white sock in the kitchen sink, along with bloodstains in the sink, indicating that the stabber may have washed a wound after killing Houston. Samples of that blood might help us identify the killer or at least narrow the list of suspects. Given that we were probably looking for someone with a nasty hand wound, I assigned one of our men to call area emergency rooms and clinics to see if anyone had come in with a serious gash on their dominant hand.

Our evidence technicians took great interest in an open pint of vodka, mostly full. There were fingerprints on the bottle, which was rotgut hooch. The price tag was all of $2.40. There was also an open can of Budweiser beer, about three-quarters full. A can of Stroh's beer was found near the victim, partially full. Two empty 7-Up cans were also found in the room.

At least, no one went thirsty during the bloodbath.

More than fifty-five other items were tagged and placed in evidence for later examination. The fingerprint guys were called in, and a homicide case file was opened.

We are on your case, Eric Houston. We will do our best to find whoever did this to you.

A GOOD GUY IN BAD COMPANY

We learned from the motel manager that Eric Houston had been an Armadillo Motel resident for only a couple of weeks, which probably made him one of the longer-term renters. The manager said he worked as a janitor for Goodwill Industries, which had a location just down the street.

His files on Houston included the name of his mother, Doris Thomas. She lived in town, so we sent a detective to interview her. Eric's mother said her son was a good person who came from a good family, but when he was drinking—and he drank a lot—he was often taken advantage of by not-so-good people.

His social circle consisted mostly of other lost souls, drifters, and human tumbleweeds who had blown into town and would likely blow out before long. Cops know this crowd better than most. Ninety-five percent of them are ripe to become victims of crimes. The other 5 percent are perpetrators of crimes.

They share a shadow world, apart from the world of work and family that most of us know. They rarely settle down. They don't live anywhere. Instead, they "stay" here and there for short durations— usually just long enough to buy a bottle, go through a bag of weed, or shoot up.

They have no options, no plans, and no clue. You would find it shocking to know that many of them have no idea how old they are or where their next meal is coming from.

Eric Houston might not have fallen into their world if it hadn't been for the speeding car that ran over his head when he was twelve years old. His mother said that after the accident, her son tended to think everyone was his friend.

The head injury erased his ability to judge character. He lost his "stranger danger" alarms. Eric had a difficult time telling whether someone was sincere or lying. His mother said bad people often did things that they blamed on Eric. He'd been arrested for a number of minor crimes, but nothing had ever stuck, so that made sense.

Eric's shady associates sometimes robbed him, too. He didn't have much to steal, except booze. He'd buy a bottle of vodka nearly every night and share it with anyone who came around.

We concluded that on the night of his murder, Eric hadn't shared enough. Our autopsy report put his blood alcohol level at more than 0.2, more than twice the legal measure of alcohol intoxication.

PROFILING THE CASE

So, we began to get some focus on what we were dealing with in this case. Our victim, Eric Houston, had some mental disabilities and more than a few bad habits, but he wasn't really a bad guy.

We talked to a lot of coworkers, neighbors, and associates who described him as quiet and gentle. He carried groceries upstairs for a woman who lived in the motel. A female former roommate said Eric was a slob and often fell behind in rent, but she still liked him.

Houston's main problems seemed to be that he was too trusting and he drank heavily in bad company, which is a recipe for disaster, especially in his degenerate circle of friends. It didn't help that he'd been living in a bedbug-infested den of the downtrodden with neighbors who were just a drunken stumble from a filthy mattress under a viaduct.

Dreams come to die in dives like the Armadillo Motel. Most of the residents were on the lam, on the make, or on the skids, wanted only by the police, their parole officers, their bail bondsmen, or their ex-spouses chasing child support.

They pay cash by the hour, by the night, or by the week for a room barely big enough for a bed and a shitter.

You and I can look down on people like Eric, but we really should thank God we aren't among them—at least not yet. Most of us are just a big medical bill, a lost job, or a pain-pill addiction away from the dark and dingy places where the underclass dwells. They aren't all that different from you and me. They just aren't as lucky.

Some of them were born into decent families. Some did okay in school. Some had dreams and ambitions. But they lost those anchors somewhere along the line. They became roadside hazards, avoided by the rest of society.

The cast-off caste live like creatures in the forest or the swamp, minute to minute, day to day, foraging for food and taking relief wherever they can find it. That's not to say they are unworthy of our sympathy or respect. You shouldn't write them off or look down on them—especially if you're a cop, because you spend a lot of time in their world.

Your oath doesn't say "to serve and protect only the people you would want to hang out with." The Eric Houstons need to be protected more than most. I tended to be more sympathetic and protective of the down-and-out because we were all they had. No one else gave a damn about them.

And so I took offense when the local newspapers buried the story of Eric Houston's murder. It ran way back in the "who cares?" section, just before the want ads. Call me softhearted, but I don't think anyone deserves to be stabbed, choked, beaten, or shot to death.

The press didn't care about Eric Houston, but his mother cared about him. She asked me to find his killer, and I told her I would.

I left her house thinking, *I will find the son of a bitch who did this to you, Eric.*

Or drive myself and all my detectives insane in the process.

SKETCH-ASS SUSPECTS

Given the dive motel Eric Houston lived in and the sketch-ass people in his social sphere, the list of potential suspects was a who's who of near-west-side slimeballs, shiftless degenerates, and ne'er-do-wells.

Eric's mother suggested we begin our investigation by interviewing three of her son's not-so-good friends. Their names were Howard Thompson, Cleveland McIntosh, and Tommy Hart.

We chose to talk first to Howard Thompson, thirty-eight, because of his impressive résumé. He had done two back-to-back stretches in prison over a ten-year period, for burglary and robbery, among other things.

Howard had been on the streets for about five years, which was impressive given his arrest record. Maybe he had straightened out his life, but that seemed doubtful.

We sent a detective to interview him, and Thompson said he'd known Eric for more than twenty years because he'd gone to school with his brothers. Howard also just happened to be with our murder victim on the night before he was found dead in his motel room.

Thompson said he ran into Eric Houston on the day of the murder while walking home from a friend's house around four p.m. Eric was riding his bicycle. Another friend who was there, Freeman Smithson (who had been drinking vodka with Howard since that morning), told us that Eric was so drunk, he nearly wrecked his bike when he stopped to talk to them.

Even so, Eric was not as drunk as he wanted to be.

"Eric wanted to party, but he would only party with certain people he trusted," Howard explained.

You may have a little trouble following along here, but try to keep up with me as we trace the drunken path of Eric and friends on the west-side bar crawl that preceded this homicide.

They stumbled from one friend's house to another, but these friends were not like those portrayed in the former television series about beautiful young people living in huge New York City apartments that none of them could possibly afford in real life. This Colorado Springs friends' tour covered a much seedier landscape, and the cast was far less photogenic.

Their first stop was at the home of Eddie Randolph, who lived with his wife and a male "roommate." Our dynamic duo, Eric and Howard, left the Randolphs' after a brief visit and strolled to the domicile of friend Johnny Oldsman.

There, Eric asked Johnny to drive Howard and him to a drive-in liquor store, where Eric, who had just received his two-week paycheck of two hundred dollars, purchased a twelve-pack of Stroh's beer.

Around six p.m., Johnny dropped off Eric and Howard and the twelve-pack at the residence of yet another friend, Bob Davis, who lived with Roberto Fasano.

Howard and Eric were packing a pint of vodka at that point, having made yet another stop at the liquor store along the way.

The party-hearty crew shared and quickly disposed of the pint, so Eric left with Fasano for another liquor-store visit. This time, they purchased beer, returned to the Davis and Fasano home, and drank some more.

Our best intel said Howard and Eric put down eight or nine cans there. Then, around seven thirty p.m., the dynamic and drunken duo left and stumbled back to the Randolph residence.

For those of you keeping score at home, Howard said he and Eric each had two Stroh's beers left as they walked back to the Randolphs'. There, they enjoyed the company of Mr. and Mrs. Randolph and the male room-mate, as well as Cleveland McIntosh, Tommy Hart, and other west-side socialites.

They finished off the beers, hung out, and played cards until nine p.m. At that time, according to Howard, future homicide victim Eric and friends Tommy and Cleveland left in Tommy's car. Their mission was for Eric to buy yet another pint of vodka.

If you feel intoxicated just reading about this, I don't blame you.

Cleveland McIntosh said that after Eric bought this pint of vodka, he and Mr. Howard went to Eric's Armadillo Motel room and stayed there for about an hour, drinking and listening to music. He said they left after Eric passed out from drinking too much.

No shit.

Cleveland McIntosh said that when he last saw Eric, he was sitting in a chair next to the stereo with his head slumped over. He asked Eric if he was okay, and Eric nodded but didn't say anything. Then Cleveland and Tommy left together, locking Eric's room door on their way out.

Howard claimed that he never saw Eric alive again after they left him at the Randolphs'. We asked why Howard stayed behind, and he explained, "I was playing cards."

I had a hunch that he was bluffing, and my hunch would prove correct.

ALIBI CONFUSION

Based on what we'd learned at that point, we thought Howard was worth checking out further. We went back to his Spruce Street home and, with his permission, searched it. We were mostly looking for signs of blood on any of his clothing or shoes. And maybe any stolen items from Eric Houston's pad.

Howard pointed out the clothing and boots he had worn that night. We found no sign of blood on either his clothing or his boots. We looked on all his other clothing and shoes, too. He didn't have an extensive wardrobe, so it didn't take all that long.

While we were at his place, Howard also showed us his "ghetto blaster" cassette player and radio, which he said was similar to the one Eric had in his motel-room apartment—the one that we suspected was stolen on the night of Eric's murder.

Our suspicions about Howard remained high, especially after we talked to his mother. He had told us previously that he returned home around ten thirty p.m. on Saturday night, the night that Eric Houston died. But his mother, whom Howard apparently lived with, said her son had come home much earlier, around four p.m., and that he'd been extremely intoxicated.

We entertained the notion that his mother might be trying to provide her son with an alibi. God bless mothers.

At first, Howard maintained that he had come home at the later hour and he didn't think he'd been *that* intoxicated. But after musing on that a bit, he admitted that the only thing he remembered for sure was that it was dark out by the time he got home.

"I must have been extremely drunk," he said. "I don't remember coming home at all."

Of course you don't, Howard. But why would your mother lie about that? Or, a better question, why would you *lie about the time you came home?*

DRUNK AND DANGEROUS

After checking out Howard's apartment, we drove him to the Armadillo Motel and had him look over Eric's apartment. We wanted to see if he noticed anything missing. We may also have been hoping that the visit might stir either his memory or his conscience.

Yeah, I know, that was way too much to hope for.

While there, Thompson did tell us that Eric's cassette deck and his cassette radio boom box were missing from their position on top of a stereo receiver, thus explaining the dangling wires. We had previously found receipts in Eric's motel room, indicating that he had purchased these items in local pawn shops.

We had rounded up receipts for a Sound Design cassette deck and a Realistic portable radio cassette player, a.k.a. ghetto blaster. So if we could track down these two cheap electronic components, we might be able to find our killer.

Over the next several weeks and months, we learned more intriguing things as we interviewed others who encountered Eric and Howard on their friends' tour. You might not be surprised to learn that several other members of this low-rent circle of friends provided a much different reason for Howard's exclusion from the Smirnoff-seeking mission to the liquor store on the night of Eric's murder.

Tommy Hart told us that he and Eric and Cleveland McIntosh left in Cleveland's car when Howard got up from the card table to use the bathroom. They purposely left him behind because he was "too intoxicated and he was being very obnoxious."

Eddie Randolph and his wife, Ruth, recalled that Howard was very intoxicated and became extremely angry when the others left him behind.

Cleveland McIntosh confirmed that he left Howard behind because he was so drunk.

"We didn't want to put up with him," he said.

Howard seemed to have quite the reputation for being belligerent and violent when drunk. We heard also that he was given to waving around his pocketknife after a few pops and talking about sticking people.

This piqued our interest, of course, but we had many suspects to choose from in this case.

A month and a half after the Eric Houston homicide, our detectives reinterviewed Cleveland McIntosh, who also had a reputation for nasty behavior now and then.

We had learned that Cleve was known to hang out in a gay bar called Hide N' Seek. We didn't much care about his sexual preference unless it somehow played into the murder of his friend Eric.

So we asked Cleveland if Eric was gay. He said he didn't know one way or the other. Cleveland also volunteered that he wasn't a homosexual himself; he just like wearing women's clothing.

"I've done it since I was a little kid," he said. "Everyone knows about it. I don't try to hide it."

In fact, he often shopped for dresses, blouses, and heels at the Goodwill store where Eric was a janitor.

We never found any evidence that Eric was homosexual or that his sexuality played any role in his murder. It just seemed that Eric had friends of all kinds. He accepted everyone, often to his detriment.

DEADLY FRENEMIES

The Eric Houston murder investigation was shaping up to be a suspect fest. His west-side crew was shadier than Sherwood Forest. And here we were with all the hoods and no Robin. Another difference: Most of these merry men took from the poor and kept it.

We entered the third month and New Year with at least forty persons of interest, and the list kept growing by the day.

The one guy we kept coming back to was Howard Thompson.

Everyone we talked to seemed to have a story about Howard threatening someone with his knife, or Howard talking about hurting people, including his supposed friend Eric.

In fact, we heard one story after another of Howard threatening or bullying Eric on the night of the murder, during their drunken stumble from one friend's house to another.

Cleveland McIntosh said he thought Howard could have had something to do with Eric's killing because Howard had a very bad temper—he had once shot a guy on Conejos Street—and he was extremely angry with Eric for leaving him behind at the Randolphs' home.

According to Cleveland, Bob Davis told him that he'd overheard Howard talking about "doing something" to Eric on the night of the murder. After hearing that, we called in Mr. Davis. He said that drunk Howard was verbally abusive to drunk Eric at the Randolph home.

We spoke again to Cleveland McIntosh on January 15, 1987. He offered the opinion that Howard killed Eric with his Buck knife. He also said he thought Howard's parents would lie to protect him.

We also had a rooftop witness who had seen an altercation between Howard and the murder victim on the day of his death. In January, we spoke with Jonathan Oldsman, who was repairing his roof around eleven a.m. on the day of Eric's murder when Eric Houston, Howard Thompson, and Cleveland McIntosh walked up.

Eric had his bicycle. All three appeared to be intoxicated. Howard and Eric stopped to talk. Cleveland kept on truckin'.

Roofer Jonathan said Howard was pushing Eric, and Eric was telling him to stop. When they began to get even more boisterous, Jonathan told them to leave his property.

We interviewed a roommate of Bob Davis, Tony Collins, on January 27, and he said that at one point during their visit, Howard pulled out his pocketknife and displayed it, demonstrating how he could stab someone.

He added that Howard had a bad temper and was known for always "bumming money off of Eric." He also said that during their conversations that night, Howard made loud references to "cutting" an unknown male who had upset him earlier in the day.

Mr. Howard seemed to have been voted "most likely to take a murder rap" around the neighborhood, but we had no hard evidence against him. We didn't even have a murder weapon. Then, in late January, more than three months after the fatal stabbing, we got a call about a man with a horse.

A mechanical horse, but a horse nonetheless.

The manager of the Armadillo Motel told us that a repairman had come to work on a mechanical horse kiddie ride near the motel's lobby and discovered a butcher knife under its base.

The butcher knife was a Magna Wonder Knife, made in Switzerland, with an eight-inch blade. We went blasting over there to pick up the knife. We were all excited, thinking we might have found the murder weapon. We weren't like kids in a candy store, exactly. More like survivalists in an army surplus store.

We sent the knife off to the state crime lab, which was so overloaded that it took several weeks before they sent their report. The report kicked our dreams to the curb. The knife bore no traces of blood or fingerprints. *Crap!*

Now, I know what all the amateur detectives out there are thinking: "Maybe the killer wiped it clean."

Sorry, Sherlocks. You can't wipe a knife *that* clean unless you dip it in alcohol. Even if you can't see it, traces of the serum will still be detectable to the forensics lab. Still, it would have been interesting to know how that knife came to be stashed under the kiddie ride.

Just what I needed, another mystery to keep me awake at night. And another dead end in a maddening case.

THE LONER WHO TALKED TOO MUCH

While we were certainly interested in Howard Thompson, other intriguing suspects kept popping up. In late January, we received a tip from an informant on yet another big talker who claimed to have knifed a guy in a very interesting location.

The informant said he was at a party in which a man named Arthur

Anaya boasted to several people that he had stabbed someone at the Armadillo Motel. That caught our attention, especially since we were familiar with Mr. Anaya and his greatest hits.

Arthur was only about five feet, five inches tall, which was several feet shorter than his rap sheet. He had arrests dating back to 1963, when he was still a juvenile. We had hauled him in for second-degree assault, burglary, motor vehicle theft, parole violation, assault with a deadly weapon, burglary, harassment, armed robbery, riotous conduct, breach of peace, damage to private property, and several other crimes against man and nature.

We learned that Arthur had been out of prison for about five months, which was a long run of freedom for him. Given his record, Arthur was long overdue for an incarceration.

We arranged for his parole officer to bring him in for a chat about his alleged stabbing at the Armadillo Motel. He proved to be an expert witness, in the sense that he had developed great skill at knowing nothing about anything.

Anaya claimed he did not know Eric Houston and had no information concerning his death, other than what he'd heard on the news. For a career criminal, he didn't have much of an alibi. He was living with his mother in Colorado Springs at the time of Eric's death. He couldn't recall what he did on the night of November 8, 1986, but noted that his usual Friday and Saturday night haunt was Rustic Hills Lounge, on the far east side of town.

When we inquired whether he had any friends who could confirm his whereabouts on the night of Eric Houston's murder, Arthur scoffed.

"I don't hang around with anyone. I am a loner. I don't have friends."

Well, at least *that* part of his story was believable.

We showed him a photo of Eric Houston, and again he said he did not know our victim. At that point, his arrogant attitude pissed off his parole officer, who got in Arthur's face and threatened to send him back to prison for violating his parole if he didn't cooperate.

Arthur then admitted that he may have known and drunk with Eric from time to time.

"But so what? I don't know who killed him, and if I did, I wouldn't tell you anyways."

We cut him loose just to clear the air of his lies. We did run a blood comparison from samples we drew from Anaya and those taken at the crime scene, but they were inconclusive.

Did Arthur's hands have scars from a possible knife wound?

I'm glad you asked. Arthur's hands looked as if they'd been through a meat grinder. Both of them. They were heavily scarred—so heavily, in fact, that there was no telling which scars were two months old and which were ten years old.

Slicing knife wounds tend to heal quickly as long as they aren't fatal.

Arthur was definitely a contender, but we had no irrefutable scientific proof of his guilt. He agreed to take a polygraph if we wanted to go that route. We then released him for lack of any proof, but we kept him on our list of potential killers.

HITTING A WALL

About seven months into the investigation of Eric Houston's murder, we hit a wall. We thought the blood and fingerprint evidence might help us nail down Howard Thompson as our primary suspect.

Our crime scene lab reports said two different blood types were found at the scene. One was the victim's. The other had to be the killer's. We had also found a set of fingerprints on the Budweiser can. They didn't match the victim, so we thought those fingerprints might also belong to the killer.

But when the results from the state crime lab came in, neither the blood samples nor the beer-can fingerprints belonged to Howard Thompson.

We had wasted a lot of time, or so it seemed, while waiting for those results, but there was no rushing justice in the Rockies. There are only two crime labs run by the state of Colorado: one in Pueblo and one in Denver, and they are both extremely busy—always.

Of course, back then we didn't have the ability to search a nationwide fingerprint database for a match. Blood analysis was even more rudimentary. So we had *nada* on Howard at that point.

Around this same time, we also had witnesses confirm that they had seen him at another house party on the night of Eric Houston's murder. So Howard Thompson appeared to have an alibi of sorts.

We didn't give up on him entirely. For all we knew, he might be the killer. We just didn't have any real proof. We had hearsay reports, from several of Eric Houston's menagerie of friends, that Howard had been bullying our murder victim earlier on the night of the murder and may even have threatened him.

It was all flimsy, circumstantial evidence. Not enough to file charges with or even to take to a grand jury.

Thompson maintained his innocence, of course. He never ever would have hurt his good buddy Eric. We didn't believe him, but we couldn't prove otherwise. This case was driving me up a wall.

My frustration had me talking to Eric's ghost at night, and sometimes in daylight. I'd ask for some guidance or a break. I promised him nearly every day that I would lock up his killer if only he would send me a clue.

We had been high on Howard as the killer, just as we had thought we found the murder weapon when the knife turned up. We were shot down time and again in this case when the science didn't support our theories.

The disappointment crushes you after a while. I'd sit in my desk chair and say, "Fuck, if it isn't Howard Thompson, then who the hell is it?"

The extreme lows and highs are what makes our work so infuriating— and so damned exciting when you finally do catch the real bad guy.

SLOW TORTURE

Months and then several years passed without anything new to chew on in the Eric Houston case. I was the supervisor in charge, and I took our lack of progress personally.

I held meetings on the case constantly, sometimes daily, always weekly. Whenever we had a bit of downtime from the daily murder and mayhem, I'd call in all our detectives and street cops from the near west side and talk through what we had, who we could look at, anyone we could check out or jab with a stick for information.

Who in this giant crowd of assholes showed the most promise as a suspect?

For the first seven months, we had liked Howard Thompson for the murder. He'd made threats. He carried a knife. We all thought he seemed like our guy, but then the crime scene evidence gave him a pass—and put us way behind on every other potential suspect.

Arthur Anaya was certainly capable of killing Eric Houston, but all we had on him was sketchy talk from a sketchy informant. Half the people in the neighborhood were capable of stabbing someone to death. Anaya was still a suspect, but he was only in the first six rows of potential suspects that we had put together.

This case had a curse—the curse of too many suspects. There were so many potential killers who knew Eric Houston. At one point, we had a list of more than fifty-two. We'd go out trying to nail one of them and come back with nothing but rumors and innuendos—nothing worth a search warrant, let alone an arrest warrant.

Every now and then, out of the blue we'd get something that gave us hope of solving this case. Those bits and pieces came in intermittent drops, like water torture.

Our homicide team kept expanding the circle of the investigation, casting the proverbial wide net, beyond the west side to the greater metro area of Colorado Springs, hoping we'd catch something—if not our killer, at least a break. We actually did a cattle call, bringing in every one of our forty-two "individuals of interest" to get blood samples and fingerprints and any additional information they might want to cough up.

None of the fingerprints proved a match for those gathered at the murder scene. None of the blood samples were definitive. About a quarter of them matched the general blood type of the sample that we thought came from the killer, but back then these tests were based on antigen levels. The results weren't specific enough to bring charges. They were only good for narrowing the field, a little.

Whenever we weren't chasing a killer in a more pressing investigation, we'd send out the troops and have them talk to anybody and everybody who might help us with the Eric Houston case.

We had spent many hours chasing leads. We'd talked to a mentally handicapped guy who briefly worked at Goodwill before being fired for suspected theft. He was supposedly pissed off at everyone he'd worked with.

The only problem was that after we'd spent days tracking him down and checking him out, we learned that he'd been hired to work at Goodwill as a temporary replacement for Eric Houston, who was out sick.

So when he claimed he did not know Eric Houston, it was because he *really* did not know Eric Houston.

We also chased down a member of the custodial staff at the Armadillo Motel who had been described to us as "a wacko" and worthy of investigating. And we spent many hours running down a report that Eric may have been killed by some white males including Lewis "Blackie" Booker who lived on Conejos Street.

We had several sources say that Howard had told them this was his concern. He said that he'd set up a robbery in which he talked Eric into stealing a stereo and cash from the men while Howard and others distracted them.

At one point, we also had some information on a suspect nicknamed Andre the Giant, after the professional wrestler. Our Andre, a big, nasty fellow, carried a knife and was known to be very protective of family members, including his sister's boyfriend, Blackie Booker, whom Eric and Howard had reportedly robbed.

Just as an aside, we also looked at a guy with the nickname "Big Head," who truly did have an oversize cranium under a very short haircut. Street nicknames can add a bit of color to a criminal investigation, no doubt about it.

There was another west-sider who weighed in at more than five hundred pounds and carried the moniker "Starvin' Marvin," even though he couldn't get through a doorway without a barrel of grease and a couple of crowbars.

After Eric's death, Howard told friends that he was upset because he thought the same white males who killed Eric would be after him, too.

Howard told a friend that he was buying a gun so he could kill these guys before they killed him.

More than two years after that unsolved murder, our detectives took another run at Cleveland McIntosh, who had driven Eric and his pal Howard to a couple of stops on the night of the murder.

In this interview, McIntosh told us for the first time that Howard had actually threatened Houston at the Randolphs' home earlier in the night. He had pulled out his pocketknife and said, "I'll hurt you, Eric."

Or so Cleveland McIntosh claimed more than two years later.

He also recalled that Eric said, "Put the knife away, Howard." And Thompson complied.

Howard Thompson was everyone's favorite suspect, including most of those who ran in his antisocial circles. We had Howard in our sights, too, but at that point, we couldn't nail down any strong evidence beyond threats he'd made and his well-documented tendency to be violent when drunk.

In December 1988, our detectives dug up a psychological report on Howard, done after a 1976 parole violation arrest. He was twenty-eight at the time and had already racked up an impressively vile record of criminal behavior. He'd been slapped with a parole violation after an argument with his girlfriend.

Apparently, she had pointed a loaded gun at him and threatened to shoot. Howard took the gun from her and then sold it on the street, which didn't please his parole officer.

A psychological evaluation was ordered up as a result. Howard's file was not boring. A native of Texas, he had made it all the way to the tenth grade before dropping out and pursuing a career as a dishwasher and petty criminal.

Then, in 1967, he enlisted in the Marines, but two years later he was discharged without honor because, the report said, he had become addicted to heroin while serving in Vietnam.

The report said Howard had been arrested in Colorado for armed robbery in 1971. He was sentenced to six to ten years in prison, beginning in 1973. He was released after only three years, getting paroled in 1976.

The psychological report said that our man Howie had severe emotional disturbances, which any of his nonpsychologist friends could have told us. According to the report, he was also self-centered, demanding, touchy, and given to asocial impulses. No surprises there. Nor were we shocked to read that he had average to above-average potential for violence, not to mention a history of alcohol and drug abuse. Yes, Howard was a problem child by anyone's analysis, but we still had no solid proof that he had murdered his drinking pal and frenemy Eric Houston.

A CROSS-DRESSING KILLER, OR A DOUBLE-CROSSER?

Cleveland McIntosh kept trying to point us to Howard Thompson, and maybe for good reason, but in March 1989, another source came forward and fingered ol' Cleve himself. He was already on our list, but not very high on it.

This source was Jessi Capperello, a popular west-sider for nefarious reasons, who had just returned to Colorado Springs from Texas. She said a Black male by the name of Dave had told her of a conversation in which Cleveland said he'd killed Eric for his drugs, cash, and boom box. I wasn't sure Cleveland was the killer type.

Jessi also gave up another bit of information that seemed highly unlikely, given Cleveland's interest in women's clothing and gay bars. She said Cleveland was dating a fourteen-year-old girl named Ashley Spawn.

We sent a couple of detectives to Jessi's house to follow up, and there they found Duane Tyler, the guy she was living with. This "Dave" was the source of her information on Cleveland McIntosh. Dave described Cleveland as "very unstable and violent."

Under questioning, Duane said he'd known Eric Houston and had partied with him over the years. Duane claimed that he'd seen Cleveland crying a couple times over Eric's death and the fact that police had questioned him about it repeatedly. Duane said that in January 1989, he and Cleveland drank a half gallon of wine and some beers together.

Duane Tyler claimed that while intoxicated, Cleveland had said, "I didn't mean to kill him," and started crying.

Cleveland had ordered Duane to leave at that point. Duane left but then came back a short time later. Cleveland then confronted him with a knife and ordered him to leave. Duane also said that Cleveland had once had a boom box similar to the one missing from Eric's motel room.

When you are dealing with this level of society during an investigation, you learn to watch out for accusers working their own game. They can be skilled at using cops to set up, smear, or scare the hell out of enemies who have nothing to do with the actual crime under investigation.

That may well have been what was going on with Cleveland McIntosh. His enemies sent us chasing after him with lies because they wanted us to fuck with him. We were their instruments of revenge.

Experienced cops are always aware of that possibility, but we can't ignore any leads. We checked out the claims against Cleveland Mac as much as we could, but then along came a big distraction: a guy who showed up out of the blue and confessed to killing Eric Houston.

A WALK-IN CONFESSION

Nearly four years into the never-ending investigation of Eric Houston's murder, I was bordering on obsession. The case was driving us all nuts. I found myself talking to the guy in my sleep, begging for clues.

Eric Houston was no saint, but I didn't run into a lot of saints during my career as a cop. His head injury as a kid made him an innocent, even though he was a hard-drinking one. He tended to trust everyone, and that likely got him killed.

I took that personally, and I also took it personally when one of the newer detectives under my guidance balked at working Eric's murder case.

"Is that the guy from the west-side motel?" he said. "Who cares about him?"

He should have known better. The other detectives in the room suddenly had to use the restroom or grab a coffee down the street. They didn't want to be injured by the guy's bloody head when I ripped it off and threw it across the room.

I tried to count to ten but decided, *fuck that*.

"You fucking idiot!" I said. "Don't you ever say that to me about any human death on our watch. If you ever do, I swear you will be writing parking tickets at the airport from midnight to eight, with Tuesdays and Thursdays off, for the rest of your career! Is that clear?"

When his ears stopped ringing and the blood returned to his brain, he apologized, and he never made that mistake again, which was lucky for him. (He actually turned out to be a good detective once he matured a little.)

I always told my guys that we are every victim's last hope. Nobody else can give them justice. I wanted my detectives to stand in the victim's shoes, and if they couldn't do that, I told them to go find another division. They could ride a motorcycle or chase drug dealers if that was their attitude.

We didn't write off any victims or any case. Our job wasn't to make value judgments about the victim. We were paid to get killers off the street.

We had to find them because they don't often just walk in and give themselves up.

Except in this case.

We'd been busting our asses, interviewing and reinterviewing every knucklehead and lamebrain on the west side year after year after year, and then in late September 1990, a Colorado State Patrol officer called us and said he had a hitchhiker who just might be our man.

The state patrolman said the guy just up and volunteered to confess to a homicide—*our* homicide. Mark Spenser, bearded, light-skinned Black male, twenty-five, said he lived on the streets in Colorado Springs. He declined to provide the name of family members, but when our detectives sat down with him, he said, "I'm the murderer. I want to confess."

He didn't want an attorney, and he had a few other crimes to get off his chest, he said.

Spenser claimed he'd known Eric Houston casually for about three years before they met up in the late afternoon on the day of his murder. They had run into each other at the Colorado Plasma Center on the west side while selling blood for cash. Both were regulars there, Spenser said.

On that day, they each had given blood, and then they'd gone to the Drive-Inn Liquor Store and bought two quarts of Miller beer. They took the beer to "the bridge," where they sat and drank it. He could not recall what they talked about if anything.

Spenser said that after they'd finished their beer, he went to a room at the Sunset Motel, and as far as he knew, Eric had gone back to his own place at the Armadillo Motel, about 4.5 miles due west.

Our confessor said he walked to visit Eric after midnight at the motel. They were both drunk. They got into a fight and Spenser said he stabbed Eric numerous times. He claimed he'd used a knife he found in the house, but he could not describe it or say exactly where he found it.

Our walk-in also could not remember what he'd done with it after the killing. Spenser changed his story on the weapon several times, saying he'd taken it with him, that he'd pitched it, and, finally, that he'd left it inside Eric's room.

He said that when he left, Eric was lying on the floor, bleeding.

Spenser couldn't remember much in the way of other details. He claimed he was in Eric's room only fifteen to twenty minutes. He said he did not injure himself or try to clean up any of the blood. He couldn't remember having any blood on his hands or clothing.

When we asked Spenser why he was confessing to this crime nearly four years later, he said he'd just decided to give himself up. He also confessed to some property damage during a fight with his parents in 1989 or so, a break-in at a doctor's office in 1988, and an arson and burglary at the Omelet Parlor in 1984.

In a later conversation with detectives, Spenser said he'd gone to the Armadillo Motel around five a.m., broken out a pane of glass to unlock the door, and found Eric drunk and passed out. He said he'd taken a knife from a place where he was staying, and killed Houston with it, but he could not recall what he did with the knife afterward.

He added in the later interview that he had taken some money from

Eric's pocket after stabbing him. He did not remember using the bathroom or leaving anything behind. He said Eric had invited him to come over and party after they drank under the bridge. Spenser did not recall taking any stereo equipment but said he might have.

Yes, we had doubts about this guy right away, for many reasons, including the fact that his story didn't match up with the evidence gathered at the crime scene or with what we knew about Eric Houston's activities on the day before he was murdered.

But like good little homicide detectives, we checked out Mr. Spenser and his entire story. We learned early on that he'd been the subject of two different emergency mental illness reports. The most recent had been four months earlier, and the other was a year before that. We had his fingerprints on file, and they did not match any of those taken from Eric Houston's motel room. We also learned that Spenser had been in the Colorado State Hospital, a mental health facility, from May 10 to May 29, 1990.

We checked the records at the Colorado Plasma Center. They indicated that the last time Spenser donated blood was July 9, 1986—four months and a day before Eric Houston was murdered. The blood center had rejected Spenser as a donor after that because he'd used foul language to personnel.

There were more inconsistencies in his tale, but you get the picture. He didn't kill Eric Houston. He was a freaking lunatic who was probably tired of living on the streets and foraging for meals. All that he knew about Eric's murder was what he'd read in the newspapers or heard on the streets from other dirtbags.

We turned Mark Spenser over to the mental health department and let them figure out what to do with him. Then we went back to work on the Eric Houston homicide, determined to get it solved or die trying.

I FOUND YOU!

We continued to hit the streets and knock on doors for another four years without any breaks in the Eric Houston murder. Cold cases like this often reach a point where the silence is numbing. We'd drive through the west-side neighborhood where most of the victim's friends lived, and we just knew that someone in one of the houses knew who killed Eric.

Why won't you tell us? How can you carry this secret so long? What are you afraid of?

We chased down rumors picked up on the streets, in jail cells and prison yards. We went back and did second interviews with Houston's friends and friends of his friends, as well as his enemies and enemies of his enemies. Of course, we did all this while also handling every other murder that came along, day in and day out.

In early August 1994, one of our Latino patrol sergeants received an anonymous tip that he passed on to one of our detectives. The detective checked out the source and learned that he was a longtime resident of the west side, who hung out in the same places as Eric Houston, including the Armadillo Motel.

We brought in the informant for an interview. He wouldn't give a name but offered that he'd been partying with a bunch of lifelong friends just a few days after Eric Houston's murder. One of his friends, who'd been drinking a lot, started talking about his criminal exploits and blurted out, "I'm Eric Houston's killer."

We jumped on that statement, of course.

"Who is this guy?"

"His name is Arthur Anaya," says our informant.

Well, well, well, that familiar name certainly got our attention.

We had interviewed Arthur Anaya about eight years earlier because of a similar report that he'd been bragging about killing someone at the Armadillo Motel. But he denied it, of course, and we had no proof, nor any way to pressure him, so we had to cut him loose.

He was gone but not forgotten.

Our new tipster said Arthur Anaya and Bobby Lee Chavez had gone to rob Houston late that night. Eric was drunk when they arrived, and he refused to give them any money. Then "things got out of hand," according to our informant. Anaya stabbed Eric Houston with a kitchen knife and then stole a radio or cassette player. We had never revealed publicly that stereo equipment was missing, which made this tipster more credible in our eyes.

But why had he waited so long?

The tipster said he had not come forward earlier because he'd heard the story directly from Anaya, who had threatened to kill him and his family if he shared the information with anyone.

The original conversation had taken place just a week or so after Eric Houston was murdered. The tipster had come forward because he felt that enough time had passed that Anaya wouldn't immediately know he was the source of information.

And, oh, yeah, this informant also had a few "legal problems" of his own that he hoped we could make go away if his information helped us catch Eric's killer.

The news that Bobby Chavez supposedly had been present for the murder with Anaya was interesting because Chavez and his family had lived next door to Eric and his family while the boys were growing up, and they had remained friends over the years.

We had always assumed that only one scumbag was involved in the killing. A second scumbag in the room might give us another set of fingerprints and blood samples to try matching with those found at the scene.

We had heard from Bobby Chavez's girlfriend that he was trying to clean up his act after compiling a long rap sheet of arrests for assault with a deadly weapon, bar fights, thefts, and stabbings. If he was running around with Arthur Anaya, he was running with the wrong guy to help clean up his act.

Anaya ranked right at the top of west-side bad guys. He was small in stature, with a criminal file that likely weighed more than he did. Arthur was like a mean-ass little junkyard dog that kept breaking its chain and attacking anything that crossed its path.

After our earlier interview with him, we had done a fingerprint and blood comparison with crime scene evidence, but it was inconclusive. The prints weren't his, but the blood was in the ballpark. At that point, blood wasn't the most reliable forensic evidence, because the results weren't all that specific.

But here is the bad news for Arthur: In the eight years that had passed since our first dance with the little pit bull, forensic technology had improved dramatically thanks to a British geneticist named Alec Jeffreys, who in 1984 developed the first practical methods for DNA profiling. Two international biotech firms, Lifecodes Corporation and Cellmark Diagnostics, jumped on the technology and filed patents.

Initially, the legal application for DNA profiling was for paternity tests, but law enforcement soon realized its value in forensics as a method to identify suspects from tissue, blood, and other body fluids gathered at crime scenes.

Once criminal prosecutors figured out that this DNA-based science could stand up to any challenge thrown at it by defense attorneys, police departments around the world gladly adopted it.

The use of DNA in US criminal cases really took off in the same year we used it—but not because of our humble little murder. Cellmark's scientists presented DNA evidence in that year's most sensational murder trial, featuring O. J. Simpson. (That wasn't my case, but if it had been, you can believe there would have been a much different outcome.)

The Eric Houston murder investigation, led by yours truly, was the first in Colorado to solve a murder with DNA evidence. But this science was still very new in those days, and to try it, we had to beat up our district attorney and wear him down to get permission—and spend public funds of about $2,500.

There were only a couple of reliable testing places at the time. We shipped the bloody socks and clothing from Houston's dingy motel room off to a Cellmark Diagnostics lab in England for comparison to blood samples "donated" by our suspects, Anaya and Chavez.

But once we had the results, they gave us enough information to confront our two suspects and make them squirm. We brought in both Arthur Anaya and Bobby Chavez for questioning—separately, of course.

Arthur wasn't hard to find. When we went looking for him, we found it quite interesting that he had just been sentenced to prison again for another horrifying crime. A year earlier, he'd shot someone with a handgun—his own niece. Twice.

Before he could get settled into his new prison cell, we brought him in for a visit and presented him with a warrant for first-degree murder with his name on it.

"I'm not gonna say a word," he said.

"That is not a problem, Mr. Anaya. We have a lot of words for you, starting with 'Your ass is grass.'"

Arthur Anaya didn't have to give us anything. He had already given us all we needed. He was a blood donor. We took samples from him, and thanks to the new DNA testing methods, we had scientific proof that his blood was found at the scene of Eric Houston's murder.

We had run a DNA test and found that blood and hair samples from the floor and the sink in Eric Houston's residence matched Arthur Anaya. Once we homed in on him, we also found jewelry and other property he had stolen and concealed in an apartment, as well as a letter he'd written, in which he said he was sorry he killed Eric Houston.

We had more than enough evidence to charge Anaya and put him away for a long, long time. His badass buddy Bobby Chavez was also headed for a cell. We matched his fingerprints to those found on a vodka bottle in Houston's motel room. We tracked down Chavez in Trinidad, Colorado, where he was working for a laundry service. Apparently, he was trying to clean up his act.

It was too late. We charged them both with first-degree murder and won convictions on both.

Obviously, Eric Houston's life meant nothing to these two cold-blooded career criminals. They snuffed it out for a cheap boom box and cassette player. I hope they got some good tunes out of it, because now the music has stopped for that pair of assholes.

I'm fairly certain Sir Alec Jeffreys never set foot in the Armadillo Motel, or even Colorado Springs, but his research and discovery certainly had an impact on this difficult and drawn-out case.

Eric Houston's life meant something to my homicide squad and to me. We kept searching for his killer, and eventually, we caught a big break, tapped into some first-class forensic technology, and put two very bad men away for the rest of their lives.

Now, it did take us about nine years, but that is the reality of being a police detective. The Hollywood gun battles and sexy-sidekick version may be fun to watch for a couple of hours, but in the end, it is meaningless. Solving Eric Houston's murder was not meaningless. Putting those two vicious pricks away was not meaningless.

Sure, the day-to-day grind of long investigations, and the hot leads that turn into cold crap could drive me bat-shit crazy, but when the prison doors closed on Arthur and Bobby, the feeling was better than sex!

CHAPTER TEN:
A KILLER PACK

THE TRIGGER: JEALOUSY, REVENGE, AND RAGE

Nevada Avenue is a divided four-lane roadway running through the heart of Colorado Springs. In the early 1990s, the downtown stretch of this busy thoroughfare was lined with fast-food joints, bars, and other businesses that attracted the late-night young and restless crowd.

Cruising in cars and packing the sidewalks, everybody who wanted to see and be seen headed to the Ave back then.

If you were a teenage girl, you probably left home looking respectable enough, but on the way, you and your girlfriends changed into outfits less suited for church and more likely to attract male attention.

Not that males of that age require any enticement.

Olympic-caliber flirting and posturing were prevalent. Guys flexed and strutted like peacocks on parade. Just the sight of so many females tormented them into dazed foolishness.

Raging hormones and the age-old competition for the attentions of the opposite sex added volatility to the scene. The potential for mayhem increased with an incendiary mix of horny high school dudes, long-haired frat boys, wannabe gangbangers, and off-duty GIs sporting high and tight military cuts.

Just add alcohol, stir up conflict, and all hell could break loose—and did.

In the early 1990s, the party atmosphere along the Ave slowly gave way to darker behaviors. Fights became more common as the summer began, and the levels of violence heated up with the weather.

In July 1991, a sixteen-year-old was shot five times with a rifle while he sat with his girlfriend in a vehicle outside the Original Hamburger Stand in the popular area. That marked our eighteenth killing in what would prove to be a deadly year.

With blood in the air and the zoo in an uproar, Colorado Springs PD assigned special details of patrol officers to cruise and walk the Ave on nights when the wild ones went a-prowling in large and lustful hunting parties.

Our guys tried to calm down the kids, but we didn't have the troops to post up at every corner or to counter human nature at its worst.

MOB MENTALITY

Even pampered pets have been known to turn vicious when prowling in packs. Neanderthals hunted in gangs, and gangs still act like Neanderthals. Cops know all too well that their fellow men and women aren't all that far removed from primal cave creatures.

Whether it's members of the Crips shooting it out with the Bloods, or fans of the Hurricanes thumping fans of the Gators, our allegedly advanced species can devolve into a pack of human hyenas in seconds.

Revenge. Jealousy. Alcohol-and-hormone-fueled barbarity. Whatever the provocation, emotional triggers get pulled, someone goes down, and the pack scatters, leaving victims dead and loved ones at a loss to explain the viciousness of it all.

The Ave was still on an angry edge that fall when, on Sept. 11, 1991, two young Fort Carson soldiers, Army Specialist Layne Schmidtke, twenty-four, and his twenty-three-year-old buddy Army Sgt. Joseph Reeves, were strolling on a Saturday night through the partying crowds.

Music was blaring from cars and bars. Hundreds of thrill-seekers packed the sidewalks and overflowed into the streets. The off-duty army buddies in civilian dress were heading back to Layne's apartment around eleven thirty p.m., after a few drinks.

These soldiers had not overindulged. They weren't trying to pick up women. They weren't belligerent or acting wild.

Reeves would later note that they had mostly talked about Schmidtke's recent return from duty in South Korea and his plans to leave the army soon. He intended to rejoin his wife, Jackie, and twin daughters, Jessica and Jennifer, in his small Minnesota hometown, where his family ran Schmidtke's Dry Cleaning.

Those hopes and dreams were destroyed in a matter of seconds.

THE AVE BECOMES DEADLY

As the two soldiers walked toward a group of about twenty-five teenagers hanging out on the sidewalk, a female in the group shouted what sounded like a warning of some kind. It was directed at them, telling them to be careful and to cross the street.

Schmidtke and Reeves were just walking by. They didn't understand the nature of her warning, but sensing the tension, they stepped off the sidewalk onto a crosswalk to avoid the teens.

It didn't matter. A muscular teenager confronted them anyway.

"What are you doing on my block?" he said. "This is our corner."

Two other male teens joined in, smelling blood in the air.

Reeves and Schmidtke did not beat their chests and roar back at their challengers. Instead, they turned away from them, intending to cross the street.

But the pack descended.

Schmidtke never saw the first punch coming.

Reeves turned and saw his friend take a hard punch to the back of his head. He ran, thinking Schmidtke was following. He did not see his friend go down.

When he reached the other side of the street, Reeves turned and saw his buddy facedown in the street and under vicious attack.

A pack of teenagers kicked at his head and upper torso. Instinctively, he curled into a fetal position, his hands wrapped around his head.

Someone standing nearby yelled, "Cops! Cops! Cops!"

Several girls and at least one boy were pleading with the attackers to stop.

"So? I don't care," one of the attackers said to them angrily. "If you want, you can be next."

Reeves ran to help his friend, leaping and sprawling on top of him to ward off the blows. The attackers kicked at him, too.

Reeves heard the dazed Schmidtke say, "What the . . . ?"

"The police are coming!"

The teens backed off. Most scattered. But one returned. He stood over the fallen soldier, reared back, and kicked Schmidtke in the head as if booting a football.

Then he ran, too.

Reeves crawled to a standing position but could hardly stay on his feet. Sirens blared. He stayed by his friend, hoping help was on the way.

A crowd of seven hundred or more had gathered around the street corner. Calls poured into our emergency lines.

Our patrol officers and the ambulance crew found Layne Schmidtke unconscious and bleeding from the nose and mouth. His bloodied and dazed friend told them strangers had attacked them for no reason.

Witnesses told the patrol officers that two males in blue shirts and blue jeans were seen running toward a nearby building. One of the officers pursued them in his squad car while the other called for an ambulance and backup.

The officer cut them off with his squad car. While cuffing them, he noticed blood on their clothing.

As he returned to the crime scene, a police dispatcher reported that this was no longer just a street fight. A homicide had occurred.

Schmidtke had died at Memorial Hospital thirty minutes after the attack. An American soldier killed on "friendly" ground by those he had served and protected.

I was home and in bed after a long night investigating another murder when the initial call came in. The location did not surprise me: the corner of Nevada Avenue and Pikes Peak Avenue.

Layne Schmidtke had died of blunt-force trauma resulting from multiple blows to his skull. From the looks of the report, every square inch of his upper body was battered repeatedly.

His liver was lacerated, his ribs were broken, and a lung was punctured. If the head injuries hadn't killed him, the internal bleeding would have ended his life eventually.

What had he done to deserve such a brutal beating? And what sort of animals could possibly do this to another human being?

A MOB OF WITNESSES AND SUSPECTS

Early reports were that we had a mob of suspects and a mob of witnesses. Our most reliable source, or so we thought, was the second victim, Joseph Reeves, who survived his injuries. The problem was, he had no idea what had triggered the assault.

Reeves insisted that he and Schmidtke had done nothing to provoke their attackers. They had simply been walking down the street, discussing their plans for the future, when they were assaulted.

There was no reason to doubt him. His confusion was as palpable as his grief over his lost friend, whom he had described as "a mild-mannered guy with a wife and two kids."

We had our hands full with this homicide investigation. We had to sort out eyewitness testimony from hundreds who saw, or thought they saw, the attack on the two soldiers.

Their accounts and their descriptions of those involved often conflicted. People see crimes from different angles, filtered through their own experiences. And all too often, they lie.

Our job is to sort it all out and somehow reach the truth.

We weren't stopping until we had it. I told everyone we talked to that we would never give up on this case. We would not get distracted or go on a vacation to the fucking French Riviera. This was a murder in our town, and we would lock up the killers.

So lie to us all you want. We will figure it out.

"We're better at this than you amateurs. We do it every damned day."

RED FLAGS

When I arrived at the scene, both beating victims had been taken to the hospital. There was a considerable amount of blood on the street—more like what you'd expect from a knife fight or multiple shooting.

Our crime scene techs were all over it, taking samples, looking for anything in the street that might have belonged to the assailants or the victims.

We had in custody two possible suspects with blood on their clothing. They had run away from us, which didn't hurt my feelings or help their chances with a judge.

As I gathered information and directed my troops, a patrol officer came up and introduced us to a third possible suspect, also with blood on his shirt. He'd been found on the street with all the gawkers, apparently unaware that his stained clothing said, "Arrest me."

I gave him the once-over, and he looked at me as if to say, "What are you looking at me for?"

Instead of indulging my urge to kick him in the ass, I had him put in the back seat of a police cruiser after inviting him to contemplate what life in prison might be like.

Next, a patrolman brought to me a kid who'd been running his mouth about what happened. A vocal member of the peanut gallery. He seemed to crave attention.

This fifteen-year-old whistle dick might have weighed 150 pounds soaking wet. He had a terminal case of acne and appeared to be hyped up on something. Maybe it was a sugar high from eating too many Skittles.

I'd go with that. He didn't look as though he could afford meth. Yet.

"What's your name, son?"

"Playboy," he said.

That wouldn't have been my first guess. So I couldn't help myself.

"Why 'Playboy'?"

"Because it helps me get girls."

I marked this meatball as a waste of time but decided not to send him packing yet.

"Well, I don't see any starlets hanging on your arms, so how about you give me some ID."

As it turned out, the world's most unlikely playboy actually did come through with some physical descriptions of the attackers, which would prove helpful.

We also learned from other witnesses that the six or seven guys who attacked the soldiers were all about the same age, but of diverse ethnicities—Black, Latino, and white—which seemed unusual. There were other reports that most of the attackers attended the same high school, which would prove useful as well.

But this would be a grinder of a case. And I would be the grist.

TALKING HEADS

What did not help the investigation was the sensational and over-blown coverage of the killing by local television stations.

The panic-inducing message blasted for months on the nightly news was "*Killers on the Loose! Your Children Are Not Safe! Downtown Is a Killing Zone!*"

Oh, yeah, citizens of Colorado Springs! Hide under the bed with a grenade in one hand and an Uzi in the other.

It really irked me.

The talking heads on TV kept calling this "the most violent murder in city history."

I called *bullshit* on that.

I wasn't nearly as old as the city of Colorado Springs, and yet I'd investigated much worse homicides just on my watch—murders that involved body parts being cut off and brain bits blown all over the place.

That very year, we had a murder in which a guy was beaten to a pulp with an aluminum baseball bat. The coroner figured he'd been hit at least a hundred times. He was unrecognizable. Every bone in his body was broken. By the time that killer was done, the poor guy looked like a duffel bag stuffed with blood and broken bones. When we arrived and saw the carnage, I wasn't sure it was a human body until I saw his shoes nearby.

Certainly, the Schmidtke murder was a terrible and senseless crime, but the television toads were running amok with their coverage.

Their reason for doing this had a lot more to do with boosting their station's ratings and their own careers than with presenting the truth to their viewers.

CAREER CLIMBERS

Can you tell that I didn't have much use for television reporters? On the other hand, I learned to respect most of the newspaper reporters who covered crimes in our city. They seemed to be doing their best to get to the truth, even if some of them couldn't find their ass with both hands.

Being a television reporter or news anchor is considered a glamour job, which explains their blow-dried haircuts, professionally chiseled facial features, four layers of slathered-on makeup, and stylish clothing subsidized by their stations.

Newspaper reporters, on the other hand, are known as "ink-stained wretches" for a reason. There is nothing glamorous about their job. They tend to look as if they slept on a park bench under yesterday's obituary section. And unlike the TV trolls, they don't get asked to host telethons or play in celebrity golf tournaments.

Colorado Springs is not a prime television market. Most of the on-air "talent" had ambitions to work their way up to bigger stations, in bigger markets that paid more and moved them a step closer to network jobs. They hyped up their stories to make them seem important so that when managers at bigger stations looked at their résumé tape reels, they'd be impressed.

The airheads on television are much more about self-promotion than truth promotion. So for them, the beating death of an American soldier in downtown Colorado Springs was Armageddon.

This did not make my job any easier. Our homicide bureau and the whole police department were already under the gun because 1991 was breaking records for bloodbaths.

Fifty cops were assigned to major crimes, but I had only eight homicide detectives, and we ran ourselves ragged that year. When the television reporters were screaming about this case, some politicians and others called for the creation of a "special unit" with a huge team of investigators pulled in from other divisions.

Here's a little lesson from law enforcement 101: You can't just transfer any breather in blue into the homicide department when things get busy. We aren't salesmen hawking hardware at Home Depot. We couldn't just pull in more help from the staff in the Appliance Department.

The homicide division doesn't have an extra-guy closet. We investigate complex crimes and make cases that are later scrutinized by highly paid defense lawyers and appeal-averse judges who like nothing more than to find a mistake so they can cut a defendant lose.

There's no room for temps in our trade. The stakes are too damned high.

THE MAGNIFICENT EIGHT

We couldn't afford to slip up or let anything slide in this case. But that was okay. We were a very tight team, highly experienced and relentless.

I was the lieutenant in charge, but I rarely pulled rank. We called ourselves the Magnificent Eight.

I was the conductor. They were the orchestra. I pointed in a direction, and they went there. We made beautiful music out of murder and mayhem that year. We worked our asses off.

We became so hardened to gore that I would order pizza delivered to the crime scenes. We didn't have time for leisurely lunches. Our backs were against the wall. We owed the victims and their families our best efforts. That's what kept us going.

The killing on the Ave was our toughest case only because of the numbers involved. Suspects. Witnesses. We could have filled the high school gym with them. This was a nightmare of a case, but if it were easy, anybody could do it. Homicide investigation can be the most frustrating and the most euphoria-inducing job in law enforcement.

Nobody wants to help you, let alone see you coming. You are on the ultimate hunt, searching for an elusive quarry—one that may even be smarter than you (as much as that hurts to admit).

Our eight-man team was made up of passionate detectives with complementary skills. Besides me (the world's greatest and humblest detective), the Magnificent Eight included . . .

The Computer Wizard, who could break into the Pentagon if we needed it to happen. (Note to the FBI: *Just kidding. We would never do that!*)

The Matrix Master, another tech-savvy guy who could navigate the federal system and track bad guys down like nobody's business.

The Interrogators, two brilliant brain burglars who could get inside the heads of suspects, reveal their lies, and pry out their secrets. They didn't need to torture anyone. They could scramble brains with mere words.

The Enforcer, a big, powerful physical specimen who could walk into a room and intimidate even the toughest criminals—but not his boss, of course.

The Locksmith, who could open any drug dealer's safe or door. For fun, he broke into very complicated pay-phone locks and replaced coins with dollar bills just to mess with the telephone-company guys.

The Bruise Brothers, our own dynamic duo of expert street fighters, who were always prepared to wade into battle if we ran into hostiles or heavy resistance. One of them, who had a dark sense of humor, liked to joke that *his* version of reading a suspect his rights would go like this: *You have the right to remain silent, if you can stand the pain.*

As leader of this pack, I tried to keep them sharp and motivated. We shared a passion for solving crimes and putting killers behind bars. The Magnificent Eight were also big on mottos. One of my favorites was "Nobody does dead like we do."

BLOODIED SUSPECTS

After twenty-four hours on the Schmidtke case, we had three kids in custody: two runners and a gawker, all of them found with bloodstains on their clothing. Once we had gathered all the information we could at the crime scene, we brought them in one at a time, starting with the gawker, Shawn Stancil.

At first inspection, he seemed like a stand-up kid, but then, mob violence often involves good people gone bad. He was just sixteen years old, with no criminal history.

Stancil was also an athlete at Fountain-Fort Carson High School, which kept coming up as a common denominator for both suspects and witnesses.

This was interesting since most of the students at that particular high school, located about sixteen miles from downtown, were the offspring of soldiers serving at nearby Fort Carson.

They were military brats and proud of it. While other high school football teams have uniforms with two colors, the Trojans of Fountain-Fort Carson proudly wear three: the red, white, and blue.

Why would kids from that school target two guys who were obviously off-duty soldiers? The answer to that question would come, but only after many hours of investigation and interviews.

Our first man up, Stancil, seemed more like the type of kid who'd want to become a soldier, not beat up on one. His father was in the army, stationed at Fort Carson, same as Schmidtke and Reeves.

When we asked him why he was found with blood on his shirt, Stancil said he'd been hanging out with his girlfriend on the Ave when he saw the attack on the two soldiers.

He told us he jumped in instinctively, to break it up.

Then whose blood is on your shirt?

Stancil said it probably came from one of the attackers. He couldn't— or wouldn't—ID any of them.

We weren't sure what to make of him. Blood test results on his shirt would tell us more. We collected his clothing and delivered it to the crime lab for analysis.

But we locked him up to keep him safe—and away from anyone he might be trying to protect.

Next up: our two bloodied crime scene runners, Kevin Moore and Anthony Phenix. Both were seniors from Fountain-Fort Carson High School and members of the football team. In fact, Phenix was their star quarterback.

He did not have an arrest record. And he came across as a decent kid who felt sympathy for the victim and his family. But for the blood on his clothing and his flight from the scene, we might have been tempted to give him a pass.

The QB was fast, but not fast enough.

Phenix claimed he'd just been hanging out on the Ave like everyone else, having fun with the guys, talking to girls, and *chillin'*, which I gather is cooler than playing it cool.

The QB said he heard a bunch of commotion, walked over to see what was going on, and suddenly found himself in the middle of a brawl. He figured the blood on his clothing flew off one of the other combatants.

He also recalled that as he stood in the crowd, someone hit him on the back, so he spun around and started swinging. He didn't remember anyone specific being a target of his punches, but he knew that the people around him were standing, not fallen on the ground like the victims.

I wasn't impressed. His story was plausible but not convincing. Again, the blood on his clothing would tell us more. In the meantime, we benched him in the county lockup.

That left us to chat with bloodied runner number two, Kevin Moore, linebacker on the Trojan football team. He looked the part: six-two, lean, and muscular.

Mr. Moore added a new twist with his rendition of that fateful night.

He was the first to admit that he'd been drinking booze that night. He claimed that he and a friend guzzled a mix of wine and beer called "jungle juice" before heading downtown.

This conveniently resulted in Moore passing out in a friend's car once they got there. Moore told us that his drunken slumber was interrupted by a friend who said his quarterback buddy was involved in a fight and needed help.

Moore's story was that he jumped out of the car, shook off his drunken coma, crashed through the crowd, and dragged Phenix away, protecting the star and playing the hero. Somewhere along the way, blood was smeared on his clothing, including his shoes.

The source of the blood on Mr. Moore's footwear was of special interest to our investigation. He claimed that he had not kicked anyone. He ran from the scene only because it might hurt his reputation to be caught at a murder scene. The Trojans linebacker portrayed himself as yet another innocent, an accidental participant in a fight that resulted in a vicious murder.

Interesting. Not one of these upstanding citizens arrested with blood on their clothing admitted to starting the fight or punching or kicking the two soldiers. They were all just babes in the woods.

Or wolves in the pack.

A THREAT LEADS TO A BREAK

My merry band of hard-boiled detectives suspected that all three were lying, but we needed proof. We knew that it could be months before we got the crime lab results on the bloodied clothing, but all we could do in the meantime was keep talking to suspects and potential witnesses, not to mention their nervous and protective parents.

Nobody was happy with us, including us.

Then we got a break. The mother of a Fountain-Fort Carson High School student called and said her daughter had information to share on the Ave killing, but she was afraid. And she had good reason to be. Someone had called her daughter and threatened her.

The caller said she'd better not tell the cops what she'd seen, or she would be next.

My, my, my, someone out there was very nervous about this young lady talking to us, which made us very interested in doing just that. But first, we had to assure the teen and her parents that we would protect them.

We offered assurances along those lines, and then Tanya Starr and her parents came in so we could hear what she had to share with us.

Tanya coughed up some useful information, but it wasn't anything she saw. It was what she had heard.

After the fight on the Ave, she shared a ride home with a classmate, a male, who said something that terrified her.

"So we killed that dude, so what?" she recalled him saying.

Excuse me if my weary detective heart pounded out a dramatic drumbeat upon hearing that.

This was a potential breakthrough in the case: an actual person who claimed to be a participant in this murder.

An uncaring, vile, and loathsome person, maybe, but one that we of the Colorado Springs Police Department homicide division would love to engage in further conversation.

In the next moment, Tanya became my favorite teenager in the world outside immediate family. She offered up the name of the classmate who had claimed responsibility for the killing and then threatened her: Dominic Perea, a seventeen-year-old senior at Fountain-Fort Carson, whose circle of friends just happened to include our three blood brothers behind bars: Anthony, Kevin, and Shawn.

STEPPING IT UP

A quick check revealed that Dominic had a bit darker past than the other three. He'd been involved in several fights, according to juvenile reports. This was another reason Tanya and her parents took him seriously when he threatened to kill her if she told anyone what he'd said in the car.

We also noted that Perea was Latino while the other three in custody were Black, which matched up with witness reports that the attackers were racially diverse, including those two and a couple of white kids we had yet to track down.

After talking to Tanya, I put the pedal to the metal. Perea had threatened her life, so we wanted him locked up, for her safety if nothing else.

Tanya had given us a good description of what Dominic had been wearing on the night of the attack. We wanted to test it for bloodstains as well. We ordered up a search warrant and paid a visit to his home.

There, we had a chat with Dominic and his mom. They prove to be tight-lipped and models of cleanliness, too.

Dominic staunchly claimed he was not involved in the Ave fight—never even saw it, even though he was downtown.

"Well, if you weren't anywhere near the fight, you won't mind if examine the clothes you were wearing that night, will you?" I asked in my nice-detective voice.

"I washed them," came the reply from Dominic's mother. "I'm kind of a neat freak."

The mother explained that she routinely picked up the clothes her son had worn, and cleaned them the next day.

She was a tidy thing. Or very crafty when it came to protecting her son.

We might have left their home feeling frustrated and concerned about Dominic Perea and the alleged threats he'd made to my favorite unrelated teenager/witness.

Except that I had a flash of brilliance, if I do say so myself.

It wasn't really a flashy flash, just a simple astute observation.

Mindful of our other suspect with the bloodied footwear, I checked out Dominic's shoes as we prepared to leave.

Mom hadn't thought of that. But I did.

Her bad.

There were small rust-colored stains on Dominic's shoes. Definitely looked like blood to my well-trained eyes.

"What's that on your shoe?" I asked in my slightly less nice detective voice.

Dominic and his mother stared down like a couple of dogs who'd been caught shredding the couch cushions. Neither offered an explanation.

I didn't give them the chance to dream one up.

"I'll be taking those for examination as possible evidence in this case," I informed them in my don't-fucking-mess-with-me detective voice.

Then I looked at Perea's mom, who was struggling to hide her distress, and said, "Oh, and I'll be taking your son into custody, too, for further questioning in this case. Let's go for a ride, Dominic."

Never in my life have I been so grateful for unwashed sneakers. Yes, it's the little things that make a homicide detective grateful, especially when they lead to bigger things, like murder convictions.

THE ELUSIVE WHY

I have been known to say that the *why* of a murder doesn't matter to me a whit, or at least not as much as the *who, what, when,* and *where.* Yet, I have to admit, the *why* intrigued me in this case.

Why would a group of teens who had never been in serious trouble viciously attack a pair of nonconfrontational and nonthreatening off-duty soldiers—especially teens who wore red, white, and blue on the football field at a high school full of army kids?

No one we talked to had offered any clues to the *why*, and that was bugging me. But then, I was all too familiar with the teen code of silence. Don't trust adults. Be loyal to your friends, even if they aren't really your friends.

Now, the other part of that code is that teens will talk to each other. In fact, they will talk their asses off even if they've been told to shut the hell up.

So I called a few teachers and administrators I knew at Fountain-Fort Carson High and told them to keep their ears open for any hallway or locker-room chatter about the latest killing on the Ave.

A few days later, the principal of Fountain-Fort Carson High School called. It was the most enjoyable visit to the principal's office I'd ever made—and as a schoolboy I'd had more than a few.

The principal informed me that school scuttlebutt had led him to a group of female students who may have witnessed the attack on Reeves and Schmidtke. He'd been told that they might have useful information.

And so I gathered these girls and reminded them that an innocent man had been murdered.

"So talk to me," I said. "What happened that night? Why did Layne Schmidtke's wife and two children lose him in our town?"

The floodgates opened. They had a story to tell that they'd been holding back too long. Their night on the Ave had turned dark when boys from their school tangled with two off-duty soldiers, they said.

At first, I'm thinking, *I know this already.*

But then the girls explained that this confrontation happened earlier in the night, and the two soldiers were both Black. It wasn't Reeves and Schmidtke. These two soldiers were in a car and they drove away.

"Okay, tell me what happened with the first two soldiers in the car," I said.

The two GIs had pulled up next to the girls to flirt with them. They exchanged words, and then one of the teen boys stepped in and told the soldiers to buzz off.

More heated words were exchanged. More teens joined in. Someone kicked the soldiers' car and invited them to fight. The soldiers weighed the odds and decided to beat it out of there.

The encounter left the teen boys ramped up for a fight. There was talk of trying to find the guys in the car and beating them. Instead, they yelled at other soldiers passing by in cars or walking across the street. The teens who had been drinking kept fanning the flames of anger, and then Reeves and Schmidtke walked right into their fury.

A couple of the girls spotted them, noted their military cuts, and warned them to walk away. One of them told me that she'd gone right up to them and said, "You might want to cross the street. My friends are in a bad mood and I don't want to see anybody get hurt."

She said one of them told her they weren't doing anything wrong. The two soldiers kept walking toward the group. The teens swarmed around them, yelling threats.

"What are you doing on our corner! This is our turf!"

Just as the soldiers turned away from their antagonists and prepared to cross the street, one of the teens punched Schmidtke. And then the mob mentality kicked in.

We knew the story from there. What we didn't know was exactly who attacked Schmidtke. We suspected it was Perea since he had a history of assault, but the girls said no, it wasn't him.

Instead, it was the charismatic quarterback, Anthony Phenix, who had no criminal record. The popular athlete was usually easygoing, the girls said, but after the encounter with the soldiers in the car, Phenix seemed to have a meltdown.

He struck the first blow to the head of Schmidtke, and then Kevin Moore, Dominic Perea, and Shawn Stancil joined him in punching and kicking him when he went down in the street, the girls said.

This made sense, given the blood traces on the clothing and shoes of the four who were in custody. Then, to our surprise, the girls added two more names.

They said Phenix had two younger friends who joined in the beating: Robert Dean and Dan Davis, both white kids. Dean was a ninth-grader we hadn't heard of before, but I had interviewed Davis.

He was the kid I talked to at the crime scene, who offered up the first bits of information on the nature of the attack. Maybe he had thought that being helpful then would keep us from tracking him down. He was wrong.

We went to his house that day.

"What's up?" he said upon answering the door.

"We're the guys you lied to about not being involved in the attack on the two soldiers that night," I said.

"I was there, but I was pulling people off of him," Davis stammered.

"We have witnesses who tell a different story," I said. "They said you were kicking him when he was down."

I waited for the next flurry of lies. This kid was on the defensive. It wouldn't take him long to crack under pressure. He didn't have the instincts of a hardened criminal, who can lie to your face for hours without end.

"I was just trying to break it up," he said, his voice cracking.

"But you kicked him?"

"Just once."

"In the head?"

"No, I was kicking his feet, I swear. I wasn't really trying to hurt him. I couldn't have hurt him enough to kill him."

At that point, I thought we had the truthful version of his role. This kid was not a jock. And he wasn't a hard-ass. We had him for assault but not murder.

"Turn around and put your hands behind your back," I said. "We are taking you in for further questioning in the murder of Layne Schmidtke."

We advised him of his rights and gave him a ride to the county lockup.

Then we went to the home of our sixth and final suspect, the youngest of the bunch, Robert Dean. He was only fourteen years old but big for his age—six feet and 160 pounds. He was a tough-looking kid for as young as he was.

When he came to the door, the first thing I looked at wasn't his face; it was his shoes. Rust-colored stains, once again.

"How'd you get blood on your shoes, Mr. Dean?"

He didn't have an answer. He knew right then that he was busted.

Without further ado, we advised him of his rights and took him to join his friends behind bars. We would later learn that Dean was no stranger to trouble; in fact, he was on probation for felony theft when the attack on the soldiers occurred.

At that point, we had six teenagers, fourteen to eighteen years old, none of them ever in serious trouble before. A couple of them top athletes and decent students. We knew that it wouldn't be long before those who were least culpable began to offer information against those who had dealt the killing blows. Teen loyalty ends when a prison sentence begins to look like a real possibility.

Bring in the parents and the lawyers, and let the negotiations begin.

Seven months after the fatal attack on Layne Schmidtke, we received the reports on the blood samples taken from the scene. The results were mixed.

The blood on the shoes of Kevin Moore and Shawn Stancil was from the victim, but the blood samples taken from the clothing and shoes of the other suspects could not be linked to Schmidtke. It was marked "Unknown."

This wasn't what we'd hoped for from our physical evidence, but we still had enough eyewitness testimony to file murder charges against all six suspects. Although three of them were juveniles, the district attorney's office charged them all as adults. The charges ranged from manslaughter to first-degree assault.

The legal maneuvers, media games, trials, and sentencings went on for a year and a half. I'll spare you the boring details, trials, and tribulations. In the final accounting:

Anthony Phenix, eighteen, the star quarterback who was identified as the individual who returned to kick the fallen Layne Schmidtke in the head, was found guilty of second-degree murder and a crime of violence and sentenced to twenty-three years in prison.

Dominic Perea, seventeen, was found guilty of second-degree murder and sentenced to sixteen years in prison.

Shawn Stancil, sixteen, was found guilty of second-degree murder and sentenced to sixteen years in prison.

Kevin Moore, eighteen, was found guilty of reckless manslaughter and sentenced to twelve years in prison.

Daniel Davis, nineteen, pleaded guilty to attempted assault and was sentenced to six years of probation.

Robert Dean, fifteen, was found guilty of negligent homicide and received a sentence of four years of probation.

There was a lot of hue and cry during the trials and afterward about charging juveniles as adults and sending them off to prison upon conviction. I'll leave that debate to the social scientists and criminologists. I think justice was served in this case, but ultimately, everyone lost, including you and me.

We lost Layne Schmidtke, who seemed to be a decent human being, whose children deserved a father. We lost what might have been very productive years from all those who went to prison. We lost a bit more of our sense of security and sanity in our world.

Mob violence to this extreme is quite rare, but it does happen, and it never makes any sense at all. They were young and driven by emotion and anger and the desire to be part of the pack. They didn't consider the consequences. They didn't think about the fact that someone might get killed, or that his death would result in their being arrested and sent to prison for a good portion of their lives.

Tragedies like this happen when people can no longer distinguish fantasy from reality. The adolescent mind is particularly prone to this problem, and in this case, they paid a heavy price, but not nearly as heavy as the one paid by Layne Schmidtke and those who loved him.

And those are the people my fellow detectives and I work for.

ONE MORE THING

There is an interesting postscript to this story, a final twist.

Because of this incident and others involving violence along the Ave in the early 1990s, the city of Colorado Springs instituted a curfew to get all those under the age of twenty-one off the street at a decent hour. One of the first people arrested for violating that curfew was none other than young Robert Dean, the youngest of the defendants and the one who had received the lightest sentence of all those convicted in the Schmidtke homicide.

And so, Robert Dean had his probation revoked. He went off to prison for three years. If he'd just stayed home, he would have been okay.

Folks, you can't make this stuff up.

CHAPTER ELEVEN:
PULLING THE TRIGGER

The title of this final chapter reflects the fact that while writing this book, I actually did pull the trigger and put an end to some*thing*, but not some-*one*. I killed my own *Homicide Hunter* television series on the Investigation Discovery channel. After nine seasons, it was not a difficult decision to make.

Don't get me wrong. I enjoyed filming every episode of the show. The series changed my life in many ways, all for the better. So I am grateful to Discovery and all who were involved, but I think we all agreed that it was wise to get out while the getting was good.

The show was based on cases I worked as a homicide detective or the head of the homicide division during my twenty-three years with the Colorado Springs Police Department. There were 387 cases to draw from, and we built shows around the most interesting ones. We were running out of material, honestly, and I wanted to maintain the integrity of the series. Fans need not despair. The show will play on in reruns, probably into eternity and beyond.

The network agreed to retire *Homicide Hunter,* but they asked me to stay on for a new show in which I serve as the host to other detectives. We will review their cases from around the country. Think of me as the color man in the booth, with the other detectives serving as the play-by-play guys.

We've already filmed the first season, and I think fans of *Homicide Hunter* will enjoy this new approach to the true-crime genre. This series will be easier on this ol' gumshoe. The cases are fascinating, and even better, I was not involved in the original investigations, physically or emotionally.

Doing the television series has generated many incredible experiences for my family and me. We've had a blast. This crazy turn in my life has brought one surprise after another.

I've reflected a lot on my career while writing this book and completing the first television series. It's been one hell of a run, and I thought I'd share a few highlights with you from my second career as an accidental television star.

GOING HOLLYWOOD

During the first season of filming *Homicide Hunter*, I was definitely the rookie on the set. Maybe they were trying to make me feel more comfortable by choosing to do my first series of interviews for the show on location in an abandoned jail.

The creepy old place was owned by the Los Angeles Sheriff's Department. The decor matched Hollywood's vision of hoosegow hell. They had me surrounded by a camera crew in the middle of a cellblock that still smelled like sweat and urine. The place reeked of misery. It was a reality crime show, after all.

So I played along. They rolled the cameras, and I began yapping away about my life in crime.

But suddenly the director yelled, "*Cut!*"

Yes, they actually do that.

I'd seen enough movies about movies to know what "Cut!" meant, but the next words out of the director's mouth weren't so familiar.

"We have a flyer!" he said.

Now, all the windows in the old jail were broken or missing altogether, and I assumed that a bird had flown in.

A jailbird, maybe?

"Where's the bird?" I asked the crew. "I don't see it."

The camera operators stared at me as if I were speaking a foreign language. So, like a rookie, I had to ask.

"Okay. Define what the director means by 'a flyer,'" I said.

"One of your hairs is out of place," a camera operator said.

"Oh, man, you Hollywood people need to get a life," I said as a makeup person dashed up and plastered goop all over my hair.

Fast-forward a couple of seasons. We were filming again, but in a different location. We had developed a simple routine. The director would say, "Roll," and I'd just yap and yap until the director told me to shut up.

On this occasion, I was about ninety minutes into describing a complex case. I had launched into the setup in the story, describing the discovery of human remains on Gold Camp Road, when the sound guy, who was new to the crew, yelled "Cut!"

Sound guys don't call "Cut." Directors do that.

"What are you doing?" I said. "And why now?"

The new sound guy looked as if he'd blown an artery, but it was worse than that.

"I just realized the cameras and the sound are not synched," he said.

Nobody moved. Nobody spoke.

I realized that everyone was waiting for me to blow my stack since we'd just wasted ninety minutes of my precious wisdom.

"Well, I assume this means we need to back up on ol' Gold Camp Road," I said. "When you're synched up, let me know when to start over."

"Aren't you upset?" asked a cameraperson.

"Would that change anything?" I replied. "Nobody died, did they? Is anyone wounded and in need of an ambulance? If not, then let's just get back to the story."

I had no animosity or harsh words for the sound guy. He knew that he had screwed up. He didn't need me to tell him anything.

Filming a show is expensive. He'd wasted valuable time. That wasn't tolerated among these professionals.

Needless to say, I never saw the sound guy again. They may have taken him out and shot him, but if so, nobody told me.

I never became one of those demanding television stars with an attitude and a posse of lackeys. Is there even such a thing as a "diva detective?"

A WELCOME CHANGE

I didn't get all pissy about screw-ups, because I truly was grateful for every minute of this late-life career switcheroo, and not because of its impact on my finances.

If money were important to me, I would not have been a cop for all those years. If I have money, I spend it. Otherwise, I don't need much. The hike in income from my television work was nice because I could do special things for the wife and kids, like take family vacations.

Strange as it may sound, doing a television show gave me back a more normal life. For the first time in nearly three decades, I could walk among normal humans and feel welcome.

As a homicide detective, I couldn't escape the sense that anyone I dealt with either hated me or feared me. I understood where they were coming from. My arrival rarely brought good news. Either someone had died, or someone was facing arrest.

Then I retired, and for seven years I drove a school bus for special-needs kids. For the first time in my life, people were happy to see me when I showed up. I could have done that job for the rest of my life.

I loved those kids and they seemed to love me—even the kid who threw a shoe at me nearly every day. He wasn't trying to hurt me. He was just showing me that he had a good arm.

Once I entered show business, my world changed even more dramatically. It was a jarring experience. I have never felt so welcomed. Suddenly, strangers in airports, restaurants, and all sorts of places were genuinely excited to see me. A woman walked up to me in an airport and said, "Did anyone ever tell you that you look like Joe Kenda?"

"Why, yes, they have," I said.

"Oh my gawd, you even sound like him," she said.

Then it hit her.

"Oh, no! You *are* Joe Kenda, aren't you?"

"Yes, I am," I said.

Now, back in my days with the homicide division, if someone recognized me like that, I probably would have taken a step back and put a hand on my gun as a warning. I actually did that once in a shopping mall, to a lady who just wanted to thank me for solving a murder.

Yes, I was that screwed up, dangerously close to being unhinged. But now I'm fully hinged. I even enjoy being recognized, most of the time.

I was walking out of a Virginia Beach restaurant when this clean-cut guy in a nice suit stared at me from across the street. His eyes widened to the size of silver dollars, and he darted into the street in my direction.

A cabbie flying down the street had to smoke the tires to avoid smoking him. The guy hardly noticed. He walked up to me and said, "Do you know who you are?"

"Yes, as a matter of fact, I do," I replied. "And I have a driver's license with my picture on it in case I forget."

"Oh, man, that sounded really stupid, didn't it?" he said.

"Yes, it did, but I'm Joe Kenda. Who are you?"

He wasn't really crazy, just a fan who was shocked to see me in the flesh.

Nearly all my encounters with fans have been pleasant, although there was one woman who became overly affectionate in front of my wife.

"If I'd had a knife, I would have stabbed her right in those silicone boobs," Kathy said.

There was one occasion in which I might have been a bit judgmental when dealing with a fan. I was staying at a high-dollar hotel in Beverly Hills because I was filming a promotion for the network.

My lawyer had an office down the street. He invited me to dinner. So I went out front and waited for him on the street at the hotel entrance.

As I stood there, a new Ferrari roared up, and a dapper guy about my age popped out of the driver's side. He tossed his keys to the valet and then went around to open the passenger door.

Out stepped this twentysomething beauty in a skirt six inches long and heels six inches high. She had a lovely figure enhanced by DuPont.

The guy grabbed her hand as if claiming a trophy, and they walked toward me.

"You're Joe Kenda!" he said.

He snatched my hand and would not let go. He told me his name, but I didn't really hear him. I was fighting with my inner smart-ass.

I lost that battle, and as I looked at his young friend, the words just leaped out of my mouth.

"This must be your niece!" I said.

My former fan turned purple.

His girlfriend chirped angrily, "I'm not his niece!"

I smiled and gently said, "I knew that, honey."

Without further ado, they left me at the curb.

Yes, I probably lost that fan, but the geezer should pick on someone his own age.

ALL IN THE FAMILY

Just as I've had to adjust to being more popular with the general public, Kathy and our grown daughter, Kris, and son, Dan, have had to make some adjustments, too. They didn't grow up with a beloved celebrity dad. They grew up with a cranky cop dad who loved them and wanted to be with them but was often pulled away by violent criminals.

Mostly, my wife and kids are relieved now that they no longer have to worry about the threatening phone calls I used to get. Or angry parents of criminals showing up at the front door wanting to massage my face with a tire iron.

The kids used to hide their father's identity to avoid being threatened by scumbags I'd arrested or sent off to prison. Now they hide it to avoid autograph seekers and people wanting me to solve their family mysteries.

Hiding is easier for Kris because she is married and her last name is different. Most people never make the connection between us. But every now and then, someone surprises her with a question about her strange old man.

Kris was teaching a Sunday school class the other day when a kid raised his hand and said, "Isn't your dad that Joe Kenda guy with a reality show on television?"

Her teaching partner in the class, a former ATF agent, interrupted and said, "Please say it correctly. Her father doesn't have a reality show. He has a documentary show! Don't you dare put it in the same category as all those fake reality shows. Joe Kenda's show is the real thing!"

I like that guy.

My son has to deal with these questions more often because he wears a name tag with "Kenda" on it in his work for the US Navy. He served twenty-six years as a high-ranking naval intelligence officer and now works as a civilian doing much the same work for the Navy.

He's even had admirals and other top officers ask if there is a Kenda family connection. Most don't believe that "the guy on TV" is his father, but they think I might be a distant relative.

One admiral scoffed when someone told him that Dan was my son, so when I was visiting their base in Norfolk, I stopped by the admiral's office with an autographed picture for him.

He turned beet red when I walked into his office, handed him the photo, and said, "Yes, I really am Dan's father!"

On another occasion, Dan invited me aboard a "tiger cruise" warship, the Navy's first nuclear carrier, for a three-day trip from Florida to Norfolk. As we boarded, Dan said, "I want to take you to the admiral's office. He wants to meet you."

This was a different admiral, and a quite renowned one at that. He was a three-star vice admiral who had been a legendary fighter pilot. He'd flown 125 combat missions and held the record for most landings on aircraft carriers.

He was a very impressive fellow, and I was prepared to be awestruck. We walked into the admiral's office, and it looked like a super-fancy hotel room with wood-paneled walls and oil paintings.

The distinguished vice admiral greeted me with this opener in front of my son:

"I have a bone to pick with you," said the ship's commander. "My wife is in love with you!"

This didn't seem like a good thing, so I tried diplomacy.

"Maybe she is in love with both of us," I said.

"Well, I'll tell you this," said the admiral, "I'm just coming home from a shooting war and nine months of combat, and my wife says I can't come home unless I bring your autograph for her!

"She said, 'If you don't get it, don't come home'!"

"Well, here," I said, grabbing a pen. "Let me take care of that."

It was the least I could do to promote world peace and domestic bliss.

Kathy accompanied me on another visit, this one to a nuclear submarine docked in Pearl Harbor, where our son was stationed. As Kathy was coming down a ladder into the mess hall on the sub, she could hear one of the chiefs telling a dirty joke.

He shut up and snapped to attention when he saw her. I think he was scared to death she'd be offended and tell Dan, who was one of the highest-ranking sailors on board.

Instead, Kathy walked up to him, put a hand on his shoulder and said, "Don't sweat it, Chief. I've told that joke myself!"

FENDING OFF THE DEMONS

I have been amused by my small slice of the celebrity experience. The greatest value from public recognition is the opportunity to connect with others, especially those in law enforcement and related fields who are dealing with demons of their own.

Other cops and emergency responders know what I'm talking about. We all carry the burden. The horrific sights, sounds, and smells are impossible to erase. I had never talked much about the worst memories, not even with Kathy.

When I was still on the job, she sat with me at the kitchen table most Friday nights, trying to pry out some of the pain. We'd have a few toddies, and I'd give her some of the details, but I never went into great depth on the real nightmare cases.

She didn't need to have those images in her head, too. No sense in both of us staying up all night, fending off the demons.

But when I began taping the television show for the first season, I didn't have to protect anyone on the crew. They wanted to hear it all, and I obliged. Honestly, I was surprised at how swiftly the raw memories poured out of me.

They turned on the cameras, and the floodgates opened. The producers and crew absolutely loved it because my stories were honest, direct, and to the point. They had no idea about the healing effect those sessions had on me.

After that first season was filmed and in the can, I felt better, but I couldn't really explain why. Then, after every season that followed, I was more at peace. By the end of season nine, I experienced a strange sort of high, a sense of elation and relief.

Have you ever had excruciating pain from a swollen joint—say, from gout or a sprain—and then taken a pill or shot that relieved it instantly? There is almost a sense of euphoria, a lightness and calm that settles in, and that is how it was with me.

It was like taking a drug that actually worked to kill the emotional pain. Telling the stories eased my torment and anguish. I am now much better for the telling. As Kathy has said, "My Joe is back."

I've been able to repair a lot of the emotional damage, and that has been a very healthy thing. The nightmares still show up, but not as often. Not every night.

So I've benefited more than I ever thought possible from doing the television series and writing my first book and now this one. I'm probably less crazy than I would have been otherwise. I'm still crazy, but I don't feel the need to self-medicate, which has been a problem for many other cops I've known.

I drink alcohol, but not to excess. Not every day, and not even every week. I avoided that trap, in part because I had friends who fell into alcoholism. One of my sergeants died of acute alcoholism. He crawled into the bottle, and it killed him. I didn't want to follow him there.

TALKING IT OUT

My greatest payoff from doing the television series was the opportunity to unload the accumulated horrors that had haunted my dreams during and after my career as a homicide detective. There is increasing awareness today that many in law enforcement suffer from

PTSD. The awareness is a good thing because it opens the path to treatment.

Still, when I speak to police groups, I note that post-traumatic stress is nothing new. During World War I, they called it "shell shock," which sounded harsh, I guess.

So in World War II, they called it something less scary: "battle fatigue." I don't think that term comes even close to capturing the torment that afflicts those who suffer from it. Nor does "post-traumatic stress disorder," which sounds like something suffered by teenage girls who can't figure out what to wear to prom.

No matter what name you stick on the mental and emotional anguish that comes with witnessing horrifying acts of violence and cruelty, the pain is real. And you can't afford to ignore it.

There are all sorts of therapists out there who will tell you to relieve the symptoms by picturing a leaf floating down a stream or some nonsense like that. Maybe that works for some people. It didn't work for me.

They tell you to practice "mindfulness," but maybe my mind is already too full of crap. I tell my fellow veterans in law enforcement, and others who have been exposed to the worst of humanity, that we can't *un*see what we've seen. Nor can we understand it or come to grips with it.

Humans are capable of extreme depravity and violence. We know that because we've witnessed the results. We are tormented by what we have seen, and we should be. Otherwise, we might as well be robots.

Some people think there is a stigma against talking about their demons. They think it's not manly. Or it's a sign of weakness.

Honestly? If you aren't upset by acts of extreme violence, there must be something wrong with you. You are either insane or lying to yourself, and I don't think either of those things is true.

Many just don't know what to do or whom to turn to. As adults, we are responsible for finding helpful ways to deal with our emotional suffering. There is no shame in that. You deserve better. Your family deserves better from you.

Maybe you can find a therapist or mental health professional who will help you find relief from your nightmares. What worked for me, more than I ever thought possible, was talking about my experiences and my demons to my wife and children and others who cared about me.

Sure, if you can get your own television show, you can do that, too. I'm just trying to be realistic here. Getting millions of people in 183 countries to listen to you for nine seasons might be harder.

Believe me, I have no idea why they listened to me, other than maybe because I spoke the unadorned truth, and that appealed to them. So I'm telling it straight now to all who carry a burden like mine. If you know someone in that situation, please pass on my words of encouragement.

We have a choice how we respond to this. You can collapse under the terrifying weight of your memories, or you can move forward. I recommend moving forward. There are resources out there, so go find them. You should be good at that.

When I speak to law enforcement groups and deliver that message, they usually applaud. They sometimes give me standing ovations. My words make sense to them, and I hope they make sense to others looking for relief.

COP CRUISERS

I am always gratified when fans and other veterans of law enforcement tell me they thought *Homicide Hunter* provided a true depiction of what we do, or did. Kathy and I particularly enjoy the annual cruise ship event in which fans of the show can hang out with members of the cast, including me.

We were docked in Cancún with one of those cruises, and we had gathered in a huge outdoor bar, spilling out into the streets. We were having a festive time when a large group of travelers from another cruise ship came streaming by.

There were more than a hundred of them, nearly all wearing NYPD caps, which got our attention. They were all active-duty New York City police officers from various precincts, taking a break from the city's murder and mayhem.

As they walked by, a guy with our group yelled out to them, "Hey, Joe Kenda is here at this bar!"

"Who?" said one of the NYPD boat people.

"JOE FUCKING KENDA!" said our guy. "The Homicide Hunter!"

The NYPD cruisers stampeded toward our bar.

One of the security guys saw them and freaked out, saying, "They can't come in here. They aren't part of our cruise!"

To which I replied, "Are you gonna stop the entire New York City Police Department? I wish you luck with that!"

Needless to say, a good time was had by all.

And I hope you've had a good time reading this book. Stay safe, my friend. Take care of yourself and those you love.

Det. Lt. Joe Kenda
Retired

ACKNOWLEDGMENTS

I would like to acknowledge the dedicated law enforcement professionals and first responders I've been fortunate to know and respect over the years. Many of them made me look good, or at least, not as bad as I might have during my career. I also want to thank my ink-stained wretch of a wordsmith Wes Smith for helping me tell my stories in print, mostly because he insists that I do so and I just want to silence the begging and pleading. Just kidding, we laugh a lot, really. Between his incessant begging and pleading, that is.

DISCUSSION QUESTIONS

1. At the beginning of the book, Joe Kenda describes his role leading the homicide division as being similar to that of a symphony conductor with his team of detectives being the symphony musicians. What are some of the techniques and leadership traits that make Joe so successful in this role? How does he approach and solve a homicide case?

2. After reading *Killer Triggers*, discuss what you think is the hardest part of Joe Kenda's job. What were your impressions hearing his candid perspective on what it is really like to be a law enforcement officer?

3. Which case in the book stuck with you the most? What were your biggest takeaways from learning more about the people involved, and how the case was eventually solved?

4. How has learning from Joe Kenda about different killer triggers changed the way you perceive criminals? Is there a particular trigger you found to be the most disturbing? If so, discuss what makes this one stand out from the rest for you.

5. Did the book change your perspective on what it is like to investigate homicide cases? What surprised you the most?

6. What do you think draws us to the true-crime genre in television, film, and books? What do you think we as humans are trying to discover or understand from delving into these cases?

7. Joe Kenda gives his honest perspective about the heaviness of the burden of "accumulated horrors that had haunted my dreams during and after my career as a homicide detective." What was the biggest breakthrough for Joe to help him get relief? What do you think we can do as a society or as individuals to support those who are struggling with this burden?